PRAISE FOR

27 Powers of Persuasion

"*27 Powers of Persuasion* offers readers some powerful new ideas on how to get others to follow you." —CNBC

"St. Hilaire provides . . . interesting and useful methods for presenting ideas. . . . He's practical . . . though he very wisely recognizes how humans think and act. His anecdotes are apt and instructional . . . and show how executives and others can present their thoughts in ways that are palatable to others without necessarily compromising or losing integrity." —*The Miami Herald*

"In each chapter, St. Hilaire and cowriter Lynette Padwa explain a rule of persuasion, share successes, and offer insight. This book is a valuable resource for current and future leaders in the workplace and beyond." —*BookPage*

"Every trial attorney would be wise to put aside his or her ego and read this book. The advice in this book will change the way you present arguments, in court and out of court, and will make any attorney a more powerful advocate." —Doug Haubert, city prosecutor, Long Beach, CA

"Utilizing the strategies in *27 Powers of Persuasion* will make you a better, more effective communicator in business and in life."

—Hadi Makarechian, board of Regents, University of California

"I hire Chris St. Hilaire for my most difficult trials; now you can use his 27 powers of persuasion at any time."

—David Batten, trial lawyer, Cranfill Sumner & Hartzog;
Best Lawyers in America: "Bet-the-Company Litigation"

continued . . .

"Inspiring, thought provoking, a masterful tool for just about any industry. The entire book had me captivated from Power #1 through #27! I learned a little about myself as I read and adapted the chapters to my own business and personal life. I've always known that you don't learn anything while talking, and now I see why. I have always said that people may forget what you say to them, but they will never forget the way you make them feel. Several of the chapters emphasize how to make others feel special, needed, a part of a team. I only wish I had this tool when I owned Heidi's Frogen Yozurt Shoppes and had hundreds of stores and thousands of employees who would have benefited from this persuasive book. It's a home run!"

—Heidi A. Miller, founder and former CEO, Heidi's Frogen Yozurt

"Everyone needs to understand the power of their own persuasion. Chris St. Hilaire's book gives readers in plain English the ability to succeed in 27 easy pieces."

—Kerri Zane, Emmy Award–winning television producer

"Chris St. Hilaire's *27 Powers of Persuasion* offers creative and powerful strategies I immediately put to use in guiding my board of directors through a series of challenging issues. Using these methods, we arrived at comprehensive solutions the team could enthusiastically support and execute. Power #27, emphasizing the importance of reflection and learning from one's mistakes and triumphs, offers a potent tool for personal leadership development. This book provides highly effective strategies for both emerging and seasoned leaders who want to implement positive changes that will make a meaningful impact on their organizations." —Tara Balfour, CEO/chair, Cranbrook Capital Advisors

"I'm enthusiastic about [St. Hilaire's] approach to persuasion, which is very simple, and which is fundamentally about positivity: making other people feel good about themselves makes them feel good about you." —Charles Purdy, Monster.com Jobs Blog

"Chris St. Hilaire's *27 Powers of Persuasion* is full of smart strategies to help you communicate more effectively. Take this book to heart and start winning people over right away!"

—James W. Robinson, senior vice president, U.S. Chamber of Commerce

"*27 Powers of Persuasion* offers a few 'I knew that' moments, with even more 'I should have known that' and 'I wish I had known that' ones . . . Not even halfway through the book, I found myself employing changes to the method and manner by which I communicated with staff, clients, adversaries, judges, and the rest of the business world . . . St. Hilaire's methods flat-out work."

—Phillip E. Friduss, chair, Defense Resource Institute's Governmental Liability Committee; seven-time Georgia Superlawyer

"Whether your audience is a voter, a consumer, or a juror, whether you're trying to convince a friend, a spouse, a son, or a daughter, Chris St. Hilaire's *27 Powers of Persuasion* has the answers you'll need to win people over. Chris has summarized more than twenty years of communications experience into one easy-to-read yet devastatingly effective strategy document. I'd enthusiastically recommend it to my students and to my clients."

—Dan Schnur, director, Jesse M. Unruh Institute of Politics, USC

27 Powers of Persuasion

SIMPLE STRATEGIES TO SEDUCE AUDIENCES & WIN ALLIES

Chris St. Hilaire
with Lynette Padwa

Prentice Hall Press

PRENTICE HALL PRESS
Published by the Penguin Group
Penguin Group (USA) Inc.
375 Hudson Street, New York, New York 10014, USA
Penguin Group (Canada), 90 Eglinton Avenue East, Suite 700, Toronto, Ontario M4P 2Y3, Canada
(a division of Pearson Penguin Canada Inc.)
Penguin Books Ltd., 80 Strand, London WC2R 0RL, England
Penguin Group Ireland, 25 St. Stephen's Green, Dublin 2, Ireland (a division of Penguin Books Ltd.)
Penguin Group (Australia), 250 Camberwell Road, Camberwell, Victoria 3124, Australia
(a division of Pearson Australia Group Pty. Ltd.)
Penguin Books India Pvt. Ltd., 11 Community Centre, Panchsheel Park, New Delhi—110 017, India
Penguin Group (NZ), 67 Apollo Drive, Rosedale, Auckland 0632, New Zealand
(a division of Pearson New Zealand Ltd.)
Penguin Books (South Africa) (Pty.) Ltd., 24 Sturdee Avenue, Rosebank, Johannesburg 2196, South Africa
Penguin Books Ltd., Registered Offices: 80 Strand, London WC2R 0RL, England

Text design by Tiffany Estreicher

PRINTING HISTORY
Prentice Hall Press hardcover edition / September 2010
Prentice Hall Press trade paperback edition / September 2011

Prentice Hall Press trade paperback ISBN: 978-0-7352-0459-1

The Library of Congress has cataloged the Prentice Hall Press hardcover edition as follows:

St. Hilaire, Chris.
27 powers of persuasion : simple strategies to seduce audiences and win allies / Chris St. Hilaire with Lynette Padwa.
p. cm.
Includes bibliographical references and index.
ISBN 978-0-7352-0451-5 (alk. paper)
1. Persuasion (Psychology). I. Padwa, Lynette. II. Title. III. Title: Twenty-seven powers of persuasion.
BF637.P4S7 2010
153.8'52—dc22 2010012523

PRINTED IN THE UNITED STATES OF AMERICA

10 9 8 7 6 5 4 3 2

Brenda, Zachary, and Gabriel,

You teach me, guide me, inspire me. Thank you.

ACKNOWLEDGMENTS

I'd like to thank the following people for their insight, guidance, and help throughout the years:

Harriet Adrian, Dave Batten, Rick Claussen, Scott Crockett, Dave Dolph, Daryl Douglas, Chris Gentile & the HCA Crew (you know who you are), Jeff Harrelson & the M4 & JI Teams, Scott Johnson, Sue Kinter, Hadi Makarechian, John Moore, Harvey Oringher, Bruce Ramsey, Matt Rexroad, Stephen Rodolf, Tom Ross, Tony Russo, Eric Schoonveld, John Scully, John Serpe, Larry Smith, Buddy Smith, Todd Theodora, Todd Thompson, Master Troung, Tom Tucker, Rick Van Nieuwburg, and Rene Zeron.

CONTENTS

INTRODUCTION

The Art and Craft of Persuasion

P*oliticians know:* You can change a conversation by touching the other person's arm.

Marketers know: It's easiest to convince people of what they already believe.

Reporters know: People hate silence. They fill it with stuff you can use.

Lawyers know: You don't ask a question unless you already have the answer.

And I know how to combine their knowledge into strategies you can use to persuade anyone of just about anything.

I make my living finding out why people think, vote, and

buy the way they do—what persuades them to choose one product or candidate over another, what makes them send one man to prison and set another man free. Using that research, I help politicians, trial attorneys, and marketers craft messages that will connect with their audience. The media plays a role in every persuasion campaign, so I've also learned how reporters practice *their* persuasion techniques on me and my clients. After twenty years, I've found that successful persuasion in every environment shares certain common denominators. Whether you're talking to your spouse or to 20 million voters, the approach and tactics are the same. All great persuaders use them, and in *27 Powers of Persuasion* I'm going to share them with you.

With very few exceptions, most aspects of life involve the art of persuasion. Whether it's the soft persuasion of getting your children to clean their room, the direct persuasion of convincing someone to hire you, or the heartfelt persuasion of urging a friend to donate to your favorite cause, persuasion is vital to your success. Nearly every human interaction involves some type of persuasion, yet despite this, many people are skeptical of it. They see persuasion as a form of manipulation used primarily in sales situations. To them, the word *persuasion* conjures visions of charlatans selling snake oil to the desperate masses, or of pushy door-to-door salesmen trying to foist dubious products on gullible housewives.

True persuasion is not about arm-twisting or outmaneuvering your adversary. Sure, there are situations where you can bully people into doing what you want, but that's not persuasion, it's coercion. True persuasion is the creation of consensus from conflict or indifference. It's about taking an idea or a course of action and creating unity of purpose. These skills are crucial in business settings, of course, but they're just as valuable in personal relationships. After reading this book, you'll see that persuasion can be both a noble cause and a source of enormous benefit to you and any person or group you're communicating with.

For the past two decades I have observed how my clients—politicians, CEOs, trial attorneys, and marketers—practice the art of persuasion. I've watched the best and worst of class in these professions, observed their communication styles, listened to their spoken language, tuned in to their body language. And I've seen that certain patterns always hold true.

The least effective persuaders tend to make the same mistakes over and over, never recognizing what they're doing wrong. They consistently reject information that would allow them to accurately assess a situation, usually because they don't want to hear bad news. They let their egos get in the way of what they're trying to accomplish, indifferent to the fact that other people in the room have egos too. They get caught in the details and lose sight of the goal . . . And the list goes on and on.

In contrast, all the best persuaders follow a few fundamental rules, which you'll learn about in this book. Sometimes instinctively, sometimes through training, these men and women grow as communicators until they reach a point where persuasion is fluid and seamless. Like great athletes, they make it look easy. For football fans, think Joe Montana in his prime; for baseball think Rod Carew; and for soccer think Ronaldo. If you're not into sports, think music. Watch Eric "Slow Hand" Clapton, who got his nickname because he makes playing some of the most difficult chords and transitions look effortless. Anyone who has tried to learn how to play a sport or musical instrument knows what a challenge it is just to become competent, let alone reach the level the masters achieve. You also know that while their talent is innate, these stars have also spent thousands of hours training and practicing.

Like sports and music, persuasion is both an art and a craft. Most of the master communicators I've known were born with a god-given talent, but they also observed, refined, and learned from their mistakes. In this book I'll give you ways to think about and implement the craft of persuasion. The art comes from someplace within, and it's a place I don't believe anyone has yet pinpointed. You'll have to discover your own innate level of persuasion talent. But whatever your ability, the lessons in this book will help you maximize it and allow you to become more persuasive in every situation you encounter.

Beyond Snow Day

I learned my first lesson about communication and the importance of using positive language when I was nine years old. We lived in a part of Southern California where it seldom rains and never snows. In fact, I had only seen snow in the movies, never in real life. One winter my mother and father decided to drive me and my younger brother to Big Bear, a small city nestled in the local San Bernardino Mountains, to play in the snow. We were elated.

It was a simple day trip. We piled into the family's red Chevy Nova and made the two-hour drive up the mountain. Near a small hill where other families had gathered, we parked by the side of the road and jumped out of the car. We built a snowman, made snowballs and threw them at one another, and slid down the hill on inner tubes. Snow was everything I had hoped for—cold, wet, and fun.

Finally we had to call it a day. With my father at the wheel and my mother riding shotgun, we headed home, talking and laughing, joking and teasing one another. My dad, usually stoic and quiet, was part of the merriment. I was leaning forward from the backseat, trying to hear every word, when the fun abruptly ended. My mom dropped what I now refer to as the "communication bombshell," committing a critical error in persuasion. She went negative and forgot the goal.

She started well. "Today was really fun," she said, but then she continued with, "Why don't we do that more often? I can't believe this is the first time we've taken them to the snow." More such sentences followed, and that was all it took for my father to retreat back into his quiet shell. My mom had popped the balloon of an otherwise terrific day. Her goal was positive—take more family trips, expose us to more experiences, take time out to enjoy one another—but her negative language didn't fit her objective. "We never" and "Why don't we ever" are usually bad ways to achieve your goal. Even as a child, it occurred to me that if my mom was interested in more time with the family, she would have been better served by a simple statement like, "That was fun. We should do it again sometime." My parents, who later divorced, never did bring us back to the snow.

Ten years after that snowy day, when I was enrolling in college, I decided to major in Speech Communication. At the time I thought I was choosing the field because it required the least math. Only in retrospect do I understand how all my choices and experiences, combined with the more than ten thousand hours I've spent interviewing people in focus groups, have helped me acquire the persuasion techniques I'll teach you in this book. But regardless of why I majored in Speech Communication, the topic held my interest. I'd always been intrigued by the way people relate to one another, and now I was seeing some of what I'd experienced personally put into a clinical context.

I learned many valuable lessons at college, but I also wondered about the validity of some of my professors' theories. Most of them had never engaged in real-world practical communications beyond the classroom. I was leery of implementing communication strategies taught by people whose own lives would not be affected one way or another by the information they spewed. They had no skin in the game. I realized that in my own career, I wanted to put theory into action.

One night shortly before graduating, I was watching a political show called *Crossfire* and debating the day's politics with a friend I'd known since childhood. About ten minutes into the debate, the discussion devolved into our usual name-calling session.

"You're an idiot," my friend said, "and you'll never work in politics." For once, instead of revising the argument in my head the next day, I decided to prove him wrong. I woke up, completed my résumé, and mailed it off to everyone I could think of in California politics. After fifty résumés, I managed to land a job with the California State Assembly in Sacramento.

It Starts with the Ego

My title was legislative services representative, but that was simply a glorified term for official newspaper clipper. The papers were delivered at 5 a.m. Monday through Friday, and it was my job to cut and photocopy every important story, then slip the packets of clippings under the doors of legislators in the minority caucus before they got to work in the morning. Think of the power! The first five days on the job were glorious. From all that reading I was knowledgeable, and by circulating the news I was making a difference.

Turns out it wasn't a difference many of the legislators welcomed. I had been making some of them look bad by placing unflattering newspaper stories about them under the doors of their colleagues. It was 1992, the Internet was in its infancy, and a San Diego legislator could easily shield bad news from a Fresno legislator, at least until I came along. Now I was exposing the caucus members to the reality (big surprise) that not everyone in their districts liked them. It made me one of the more unpopular new hires in the state capitol.

I was promptly pulled into my supervisor's office and shown the error of my ways. "No more bad news," I was instructed. As most hungry young staffers would, I apologized and stopped clipping the bad news, but the lesson from that experience was indelibly etched into my mind. It appears in this book as Power #9, "Recognize Their Reality." If you hope to persuade people of something, it's absolutely crucial that you stay receptive to all the pertinent information. Shielding yourself from bad news doesn't make it less true, it makes you oblivious. This is a major reason politicians lose elections, lawyers lose trials, and automakers claim bankruptcy at the expense of the American taxpayer.

Throughout this book, I'll ask you not to be the average politician or car company executive. I'll ask you to stay open to all the available information. Understanding what your friends and colleagues think about you and your goals is essential to growing as a communicator. Never hide from the news, personal or public.

A few years after my apprenticeship in the state legislature, I was able to more fully understand why the caucus members, and most people, are so poorly equipped to handle bad news or criticism. It threatens our egos. Most of us are aware of the ego in the Western sense of the term, as a part of our psychological makeup that has to do with self-esteem. Eastern philosophies such as Buddhism have a different concept. The Eastern perspective holds that a tension exists in all of us: the battle between the ego that says, "I'm different. I'm special," and the higher spirit that knows, "We're all the same. We're one." In Powers #2 and #3, I'll describe this in greater detail, because understanding the Buddhist view of the ego is central to being able to use the powers in this book.

I officially converted to the philosophy of Buddhism in my late twenties. I wasn't unhappy with the Catholic faith in which I was raised, but I was bothered by what I perceived as its inconsistencies. This is by no means an indictment of it or other Western religions. My wife is a devoted Catholic, and we got married in a Catholic church (with Buddhist chanting as part of the ceremony). However, Catholicism wasn't the right fit for me and didn't fill the void I felt a religion should.

Buddhism did. I've learned much about communication from one particular Buddhist teacher, Master Hang Truong. While I will only occasionally mention him by name, many of his insights are incorporated into the 27 powers.

From Campaign to Courtroom

After about a year in the State Assembly Caucus, I made the jump to political campaigns. There I learned the importance of language, of choosing each word with meticulous care. I learned how success or failure is determined by your campaign's ability to capture the public sentiment and define the language and terms being used. As I'll discuss in Power #12, "Own the Language," I figured out that the reason we don't have more school choice programs in America is because (policy wonks on both sides cringe) everyone calls them *vouchers*. It's a language issue, and school choice advocates have lost the language battle, at least for now.

I spent several years as a political consultant working on campaigns ranging from U.S. Senate to state initiatives, but eventually I grew tired of the power grabs and drama of it all. While it's true that there are politics in any industry, the personal nature of behind-the-scenes "political politics" was taking a toll on my passion for the fight. As I was pondering where else I could focus my political marketing expertise, I heard about a group of businesspeople who were forming a PAC to try to change the direction of the GOP—to make it more inclusive and less interested in social litmus tests to define what a "good Republican" was. They were looking for a political director, and I jumped at the opportunity. The members were entrepreneurs, CEOs, and lawyers. Over the next three years I taught them the communication strategies of the political arena, and I learned many of the strategies of the business world.

During my time with the group, I occasionally observed prominent trial lawyers in action, working the room at events. Most of them had a remarkable ability to connect with people. One day I asked one of these attorneys, "How do you decide what to tell a jury? How do you establish a winning argument?" His answer astonished me.

He said that most legal arguments were based on gut instinct, a combination of intuition and experience. I was amazed that anyone would go into a trial—essentially a message campaign—with only instinct as a guide, especially when millions of dollars were on the line. He then told me that for high-stakes cases, lawyers sometimes did do research in the form of mock trials. In those, a group of attorneys would present their case to mock jurors, with lawyers from the same firm playing the role of opposing counsel. After the mock trial, the attorneys would ask the jurors how they felt about what they had heard.

This "tell them our story and see what they think" approach was the opposite of how we developed messages for political campaigns. In those, we first conducted focus groups to learn how voters perceived an issue or candidate. Then we created a message that aligned with the audience's existing perceptions. Last, we chose the best messenger to deliver our message. Sometimes we used a consumer group or a well-respected individual. In other cases an average citizen was the best messenger. And in certain campaigns, a statistic or an award worked best to bolster our credibility and help us make our point. (You'll read about all these and more in the 27 powers.)

In the mock trials, attorneys were delivering their argument (the message) without ever having asked the jurors how they perceived the facts of the case. If they didn't understand the jurors' reality, how could they know which argument would ring true to them, or who would be the best messenger (attorney or witness) to deliver it?

That's when it hit me for the first time: *Whether the arena is personal, political, or the courtroom, the fundamentals of effective persuasion are always the same.*

I took the techniques that worked in political and marketing campaigns and began to offer legal teams the same type of research. I delivered the identical presentation I had been making for years, except this time I inserted the word *juror*:

- Jurors [Consumers/Voters] want a consistent story.
- Jurors [Consumers/Voters] want a simple story.
- Jurors [Consumers/Voters] don't care until it affects them.
- Jurors [Consumers/Voters] don't care about the details.
- Jurors [Consumers/Voters] want the big picture.

Our methods were unique to jury consulting, where the experts usually hailed from the fields of psychology or sociology. Conducting market research in order to develop a legal argument had never been done before. From our very first trial, the approach succeeded. In the ten years since, our research with mock jurors has provided me with crucial pieces of the persuasion puzzle.

It turned out that in major litigation, a big obstacle to creating effective messages was that the lawyers knew too much about their cases. Attorneys often spend years "working up" a case before it goes to trial, delving into the most minute legal details. Ninety-seven percent of these cases settle out of court, but for the 3 percent that go to trial, the lawyers' depth of knowledge creates a problem. They must present their case to a group of jurors who have no legal training, most of whom don't want to be there in the first place. And many lawyers don't know how to simplify the message.

Jurors are tasked with deciding whether or not a "burden of proof" has been met, but what they really ask themselves—the question that is debated in the deliberation room—is "Who is right and who is wrong?" They want a protagonist and an antagonist, like they get in a great novel or film. They don't want a case, they want a good story, as you'll read about in Power #11, "Keep It Simple." When jurors discuss their decisions after a trial, "fairness"—not the law—is what they talk about. If the story gets too complicated, if there is too much legalese and detail, the jurors will simplify the case until it is a story to which they can apply their version of fairness. Telling a strong, simple story that fits in with the jurors' perception of fairness is what makes a winning legal argument.

Persuasion by Another Name: The Pitch, the Angle, the Argument, the Spin

I often get questioned about whether or not it's right to "alter" a case to fit a jury's predispositions. Let me be clear: We are not changing the facts or misleading anyone. That's not what we do. But if everyone agreed on the facts, there would be no lawsuits in the first place. Plaintiffs and defendants have different views of what the facts are, and it's important to understand which facts your jury is interested in knowing more about. I would argue that it is incumbent upon attorneys to find out what a jury wants to know, because it's not fair to expect them to decide a case without having heard answers to their questions.

I have watched lawyers argue facts jurors aren't interested in learning, and more often than not, the result is that the jurors stop paying attention. Sometimes they actually doze off. Every day, cases are decided on issues that neither lawyer argued. Jurors insert their biases into the case based on their personal experiences and understanding. Addressing those biases makes all the difference in trial outcomes. At my firm, Jury Impact, we uncover juror biases and find ways to address, redirect, and assuage them. My other firm, M4 Strategies, does the same for consumer and political clients. In all those areas as well as in personal relationships, people's biases shape their perception.

One case sticks in my mind as an example of how differently people can view the same product, cause, or candidate. M4 Strategies was conducting focus groups for a potential candidate for a congressional seat in Southern California. A self-made millionaire, this man had both the financial resources and the personal drive it takes to win a crowded primary. During our due diligence phase (when we determine whether or not the candidate is electable), we assembled two focus groups of twelve voters and presented them with information about our candidate. Sitting behind a one-way mirror, I listened as the moderator outlined the man's biography. He talked about the candidate's business and philanthropic work, his education and family background, and he mentioned that he had a wife and four sons, ages thirty-one, twenty-seven, eight, and five.

What was the first question from the women in the group?

"How many times has he been married?"

They wanted to know whether or not he'd left his first wife after he'd made it big in business. Women picked up on something the male candidate, three male consultants, and the male moderator had not: The age disparity of the children meant that this was his second marriage. Next question?

"What does she look like?"

What they really wanted to know was whether or not the second wife was a "trophy wife." Voters look for code words. They look for clues into character. They want to know the little details that, based on their biases, tell them about the larger issues. The women in the group were putting themselves in the shoes of the first wife. With almost no information, they surmised a whole lot about the situation—and at least partially, they were on the right track.

People see the world differently based on their gender, their social situation, their ethnicity, religion, job, and so forth. Those factors create stereotypes, and the stereotypes drive perspectives about every single situation they encounter. We all develop opinions quickly and then do our best to confirm them. The clinical term is "confirmation bias." As I'll discuss in Powers #6 and #7, this makes first impressions critical.

Some facts are indeed irrefutable—the plane crashed, the money is missing, the man is dead. But in most situations, the truth is not straightforward. Truth depends on perspective, and that's why there's disagreement. That's why there are competing candidates, products, and trial lawyers. It is also why there are competing news outlets and editorial slants. So when people ask me about "altering" a case, I remind them that putting your story into the appropriate perspective is fundamental to any victory. In politics it's called spin. In journalism it's called the angle. In advertising it's called the pitch, and in the courtroom it's called the argument. They are all words for the same thing: a message that tells your story in the most persuasive way.

How to Read This Book

The 27 powers that follow were selected because each of them can be used in any persuasion situation. The techniques cut across all industries and are just as reliable in personal relationships. As I mentioned earlier, the powers are informed by the observations and wisdom of my Buddhist teacher, Master Hang Truong, a man I have come to respect as much as anyone I know. The book was designed to be read through the first time from beginning to end. Once you've done that and understand the foundation, each of the chapters stands on its own. You can dip into the book wherever you like, focusing on whatever powers meet your needs on a given day.

The first five chapters cover the basics of my approach,

from understanding the ego to grasping group dynamics. You'll learn, for instance, that stating a goal out loud makes you the leader even if you're not officially the one in charge. You'll learn that a person who feels threatened by you will never be open to your ideas, so the first step in a meeting is to make everyone feel safe. I'll teach you the best way to handle difficult egos, and the conversation clues that reveal whether a person feels safe or insecure. Equally important, you'll discover how to honestly assess your own ego, and how to make your weaknesses your strengths.

The purpose of true persuasion is not to conquer but to unite. The remaining powers focus on the strategies that will help you achieve this. I'll teach you how skilled persuaders use the right words, numbers, and advocates to make their case. You'll learn how to use silence and touch to steer a conversation and get people to open up. I'll show you the most effective way to deal with opposition, to challenge bad ideas, to change your goal while maintaining momentum, and much more.

As you're reading, you'll notice that some of the powers overlap and are mentioned in more than one chapter. This is intentional, because the powers work together and reinforce one another. You'll probably never be in a meeting where you use all 27 powers, but as you grow more comfortable with them, you'll see how easily they mesh. It's like learning a language. With practice, you'll become fluent, and the techniques will become a natural part of your conversation.

These 27 powers are the strategies practiced by America's best persuaders, and now they are yours as well. As with any tool, their value depends on the person using them. You can use a car to rush a child to the hospital, to win a race, or to cruise down the highway. You can also use a car to commit a crime. It's the same with the 27 powers of persuasion. They'll take you wherever you choose to go, so choose carefully.

As I sit here in Park City, Utah, in our little vacation home at the base of Main Street, I can't help but think back to my family's one and only visit to the snow. Thirty-two years later, both literally and figuratively, I've found my place in the snow. I hope the lessons in this book will teach you to become a better communicator and will help you find your place in the snow too.

Chris St. Hilaire

January 2010

POWER #1

Focus on the Goal

Whenever I meet with a new client, the first thing I say is, "You know too much about your business." Lawyers know too much about the details of a case, and they lose track of the overarching themes. Politicians know too much about policy and legislation, and they lose track of the issues that matter to voters. Businesspeople spend hours on schedules and budgets and marketing plans, not realizing that everyone in the company knows too much about their particular slice of the business, and therefore everyone has a different perception of what they are trying to achieve.

In each of these cases, people lose sight of the goal and get stuck on the process.

"Process" is everything you do to achieve a goal—all the ideas, meetings, paperwork, and steps it takes to get there. These things are necessary, of course, but they become distracting and frustrating if they don't relate to the goal. Think about your last conversation with a computer technician. You tell him, "I press this button and it doesn't turn on," and he immediately launches into a lecture about gigabytes and hard drive and bandwidth, and you want to grab the cord of the computer, throw it over the nearest door, and hang yourself. Because you don't care. You don't want to know about the process of fixing your computer, you want to know if he can help you achieve your goal of turning it on so you can print your document or access the Net.

Whenever you're trying to persuade, your first mission is to define the goal. The most effective way to do this is not to announce the goal to the group, but to help everyone decide on it together. You want to have the largest possible buy-in from everyone involved, and you get it by having everyone contribute to the goal at the beginning. This is true whether you're deciding on the menu for the holiday party or the products to produce for the coming year.

A good way to get the ball rolling is to simply ask the room,

"What's our goal? What are we trying to accomplish today?" Let people talk. Let them give you the answer. If someone doesn't speak up, directly ask that person for input. Boil the goal down to one or two simple sentences that everyone agrees on, even if it seems obvious. There is great power in stating the obvious. No one wants to do it, because it seems so rudimentary, but the minute you state the "obvious" goal of a meeting, you become the leader even if you're not officially in charge. This is because every group has an innate longing to be unified. Confusion and discord make people feel anxious and threatened, and unity makes them feel safe. People unify around a goal.

I experience this phenomenon nearly every day, but the best example of it was the time I was hired by a health insurer to help figure out why insurance companies have a negative reputation. (You're probably thinking you could tell me the answer right now.) At our first meeting, I sat at the table with the chief executive officer, the chief financial officer, and the chief marketing officer and asked them a very simple question: "What is insurance?" Each man had a completely different answer. Granted, insurance is complicated. But if the people in charge of a product can't agree on its definition, how can they explain it to others, let alone persuade the public that the product is worthwhile? After talking it through for a couple of hours, we all agreed that the goal of insurance is to predict, quantify, and manage risk. If that seems completely obvious to you, then I've proved my point: Sometimes the most obvious situations are the least clear to the people most deeply involved in them. Be the person who asks the obvious questions and says, "What's the goal here?" and you'll be in the best position to lead and persuade the room.

POWER #2

Evaluate Egos

In order to persuade, you have to understand the people you're persuading. At the most basic level, that means understanding how the ego works and learning to recognize when someone is feeling threatened. A threatened person is not going to be open to your ideas, which is why many of the powers in this book are geared toward making people feel safe and included. So you must learn to identify who is feeling safe and who is not. You are part of the dynamic, so you have to pay attention to your own ego too.

When people in the West talk about ego, they're usually referring to a static condition—"She's an egomaniac," or "He's got no ego when it comes to sharing credit." The Eastern view is more fluid. It's about the push and pull between ego and spirit. Eastern philosophers believe that inside each of us, at all times, is a struggle between the ego that says, "I'm different. I'm special," and the spirit that knows, "I'm just like everyone else. We're all the same." The spirit tells you, "She has kids, I have kids, we probably share the same concerns." The ego tells you, "Buy a new car, make lots of money, buy a big house, you're better than the others." There's nothing wrong with big houses and nice cars. But when you tell yourself that you're better, you usually end up feeling distant and separate. The ego creates a wall between you and others; the spirit wants to connect. The ego is fear-based and usually accompanied by insecurity.

Once you're aware of the struggle between your ego and your spirit, it frees you. Instead of being driven by your ego, you can recognize it and consciously decide whether to act from ego or from spirit. When you're trying to persuade people, coming from the spirit—from a place of unity and inclusion—is more effective.

Before entering a setting where you're hoping to persuade, it's a good idea to evaluate the egos that will be in the room, starting with your own. Think about the conversation you're about to have and try to pinpoint the parts of it that make you nervous. Maybe you're about to ask your supervisor for three new employees and you're secretly worried that even if she agrees, you won't be able to meet your production quota. Or maybe you're about to ask your team to contribute one weekend a year to a local food drive and you're afraid they'll resent it. Those are the areas where your ego is most vulnerable and might cause you to be defensive instead of receptive to other people's input. You need to be aware of the fear so if it gets activated during your conversation, you can manage it strategically, not emotionally.

Then spend a few minutes thinking about each person you'll be persuading. Was your last encounter friendly or confrontational? Do you consider the person an ally or a threat? The people who threaten your ego are typically those who in the past have made you look bad (by publicly attacking you or failing to support you) or feel bad (by judging you unfairly, betraying you, or foisting work on you). Sometimes they're simply the people who intimidate you. When that's the case, remember that everyone has an ego. You're in a better position to persuade people who threaten your ego if you can step back from your negative feelings and try to neutrally acknowledge the history you have with the person.

To evaluate other people's egos, you can start by realizing that when they walk into the room, their biggest concern will be how you will make them feel. Will you ask their opinion or ignore them? Lighten their load or ruin their week? If they're management, they'll want to look good in front of their boss. If they're workers, they'll want to look good in front of management. This applies to everyone from the CEO down. People tend to assume that those in positions of power are always confident, but they're not. No one is immune to feeling insecure.

Throughout the conversation, whether they are conscious of it or not, your listeners will be shifting between feeling threatened and feeling safe. My teacher, Master Truong, explains it this way: "All minds have a state of being 'open' and 'closed.' It doesn't happen quickly, like hands clapping, but slowly, like a shell slowly opening and closing. At any moment in our conversation we always shift from one side to the other, open and closed. If you can detect the moment when a person shifts to a more open state, that's a good time to offer your opinions."

Whoever you're dealing with, conversation clues will help you get a sense of that person's ego and state of mind, open or closed. People whose egos are secure tend to be outwardly focused and aware of how the language they use affects others. They'll ask how you are and will seem to really care about your answer, because they probably do care. They will ask for your input, and they won't interrupt you as you're giving it. They know how to listen. Your gut reaction to people who do these things is to like them. You might not even realize *why* you like them, you'll just think, "He's a really nice guy." If you dissect the conversation, you'll realize that you liked this person because he or she made you feel valued and included.

You can also use conversation clues to figure out which people are not secure, and it's usually pretty obvious. Do they say "I" a lot? Do they put other people down? Do they want to dominate the discussion? Do they interrupt? Is their speech generally negative? Do they use a lot of "buts"? Do they brush aside the opinions of others? These people may seem intimidating, but underneath it they're insecure. That's the piece of information you need to be aware of if you want to persuade them.

In any group, the people who know how to make others feel included are the people whose opinions you should be most concerned with, because everyone else is going to gravitate toward them. They understand the ego, whether they call it that or not, and they know that everybody wants to belong. One of the reasons they have power is because they've figured this stuff out. They'll recognize when you're using the strategies I teach in this book, and that's good, because it puts you on equal footing with them.

CEOs are often masters at managing egos. Some of the best CEOs almost seem to have what's typically called female intuition—they can pick up on the emotion of the group and use it to their advantage. However, some CEOs have one major blind spot: themselves.

I first noticed this years ago when I was hired to strategize for a political campaign in Southern California. The behind-the-scenes effort was jointly founded by three local CEOs who will have to remain anonymous. The three men—let's call them Steve, Phil, and Joe—and I spent many weeks together. I was low man on the totem pole, and they quickly began to relax around me. Whenever one of the three left the room, the other two would talk about him. After about a week I decided to engage in a little experiment. When I was alone with Steve, I said, "Have you ever noticed how insightful some people are about everyone except themselves?"

"You know, you're right! That's Phil and Joe exactly!" he said.

I did the same thing with Phil and with Joe, and got the same response from each of them. Individually, they recognized that the *other* two were very perceptive about everyone except themselves. And they were all correct: None of them was self-aware.

It struck me that the person who could make the others

feel good, who could put aside his own ego and focus on the goal, could actually be the most effective person in the room. There are different power positions within any room, but the point remains that once you understand the nature of the ego, you can be more persuasive because you know how to play to it. You become a third-party observer of the group's dynamics, even when you're a member of the group. If you can set aside your own ego and effectively manage the others', you put yourself in a great position of control.

POWER #3

Soothe or Sidestep Other Egos

You can't persuade until the other person is open to being persuaded. To reach this point, you need to make people feel safe and accepted so they will be open to your ideas, as we mentioned in Power #2. In some situations you may need to deal with the egos of people who feel threatened by you. This can happen when you're a new addition to a group (like a new employee or an outside consultant), when you're dealing with someone who's particularly insecure, or when you find yourself on the opposing side of an issue. The best strategy in these circumstances is to either soothe or sidestep the other ego. In doing so, you'll be showing those who are threatened that you are on their side; you'll be reminding them of your common goal; and you will be using language that validates their position.

One of the easiest ways to soothe an ego is to use the phrase "From my perspective." What you're really saying is, "You can have a perspective too. We're all equal here." Whether people feel threatened or not, that phrase takes care of their egos because it's value-neutral. *Perspective* is an incredibly useful word that implies you're going to take the emotion out of the conversation, and that makes everyone relax a little bit.

Sometimes you have to be more specific with your ego-soothing strategy. This is often the case when my team and I are working with corporate legal teams. Many times, the chief executive brings us in to help shape a message after the corporate attorneys have lost a case and it's headed for appeal. The execs are panicking because they're not sure their legal team can win, and millions of dollars are at stake. So we walk into the room with a very anxious client and a group of attorneys whose egos are already bruised from having to use our services in the first place. After we have introduced ourselves and before we get down to the nitty-gritty of the case, I'll tell the attorneys, "I know you have the toughest job in the room. I get the easy part. I get to give you advice. If it works, I get credit. If it doesn't work, I get to say, 'They didn't follow our advice perfectly.' You have to argue the case in front of a jury. That's why your job is the hardest. I understand that, and I'm here to support you."

This speech, which is very sincere on my part, does the trick every time and for any client. I can say, "You have the toughest job—you have to report to the stockholders," or "You're the person whose credibility is on the line because it's your name on the ballot." After I say that, I'll see them sigh a little bit, and I know they're thinking, "Okay, he gets it." Then I can continue, "To a lesser extent, my credibility is on the line too. And so what I'm thinking is . . ." Now we're on the same side, in it together.

One way to soothe the egos of powerful people is by boosting them, then transitioning to your own point about how to help them accomplish their goal. Most people assume CEOs and other power players already know how brilliant they are and don't need their egos boosted. Not true. I know from experience that the folks in power are often more insecure than anyone else. Don't try to fake enthusiasm for their ideas, because they're usually very perceptive and will know you're trying to snow them. However, if some part of their plan really is good, you can honestly compliment them and then transition to your own idea: "That was a great strategy you just came up with. Here's what I liked about it . . . and here's another way to look at it."

Along the same lines, when boosting a big ego, it helps to try to look at the situation purely from that person's perspective. Everyone has a need, and with a little research you can usually discover what that need is and come prepared with a suggestion that will meet it. At the very least you'll impress the person with the extra effort you've put in.

Every now and then, you'll need to persuade someone who is extremely insecure and intent on establishing his or her dominance. You may or may not know this about the person before you walk into the room, but within the first five or ten minutes you'll figure it out. The most effective way to handle a big, insecure ego is to sidestep it.

The best response is usually no response. If the person says, "That client is not going to open up to anyone but me," and you're itching to reply, be aware that responding will only make *you* look insecure too. The egotistical person will always be viewed more negatively, and the room will always side with the unifier. If you confront the person, the group will be forced to choose between two big egos and you'll lose your advantage.

The language to use when sidestepping a big ego is always a version of "Everyone's got a good opinion. Even if we don't follow it, we should listen to it." If the person says, "I've been on the front lines for twenty years and I'm the best person to make this decision," you can sidestep it with "I think new opinions and experienced opinions are both important, and the best decisions are a combination of the two." That's a unifying theme, and everybody's going to gravitate to the person who unifies more than they are to the guy with the big ego.

Occasionally powerful people with large egos gain insight about themselves and decide to change. In a *60 Minutes* segment aired in April 2009, hotelier and casino mogul Steve Wynn made a surprising confession to interviewer Charlie Rose. Rose prefaced the remarks in a voice-over: "Steve Wynn is known for his charm, but he's also known for his explosive temper." Then Wynn explained, "I wish that I was a more considerate person and to the extent that I demonstrate consideration for other people at my age, I wish that I had gotten to that point earlier." Wynn's friendship with the Dalai Lama helped him curb his temper and his ego—or at least raised his consciousness about it. Wynn says the Dalai Lama told him, "When you get angry, when you lose your temper . . . [when you] shout and react in a poor way to other people, it is a result of a false sense of yourself, an inflated sense of yourself that is worthless."[1]

People with big egos are usually aware of it when their behavior is becoming unseemly. Steve Wynn knew his temper was a problem or he wouldn't have told that story on *60 Minutes*. That's why, if you're around a large ego who is becoming irrational or angry, the best response is often no response. You don't cower, but you don't fight. You just let it be. By not letting it affect you one way or the other, you're sidestepping it and allowing it to burn out on its own. In the end, the big ego will respect you more for it.

Sports stars are notorious for their supersized egos. Anytime you hear someone talking about himself in the third person—a habit of some A-list players—you know you're in the company of a large ego. You can't really blame the young players. They don't have the sophistication of a corporate CEO who's spent twenty years climbing the ladder and learning along the way. They're twenty-two and getting handed $10 million and told, "Go for it." No wonder they think they're god. But even with egos like these, the skilled persuader knows how to connect.

Scoring a Home Run with a Legendary Ego

Anne Doyle was one of the nation's first women to work as a reporter and anchor in television news and sports. The daughter of Detroit sports broadcaster Vince Doyle, Anne spent many an instructive season sitting next to her dad in the press box. From 1978 to 1984, she covered sports on air for CBS-TV's Detroit affiliate.

"This was at a time when it was brand-new for women moving into those fields," recalls Anne. "I was dealing with the whole discomfort of a woman being in that job, whether it was covering news, or approaching athletes out in the field, or going into a locker room and interviewing them there." In fact, Detroit Tigers general manager Jim Campbell had warned Anne, "Over my dead body you'll go in our Tiger clubhouse." Less than six months later, a federal court in New York ruled that sports teams couldn't continue to discriminate against female sports reporters by keeping them out while their male competitors went into the locker rooms. Anne took full advantage of the ruling. She was not always welcome.

"I didn't have any role models, and the male athletes had no experience with how to act with women reporters. They had really conflicted feelings about whether I should even be there, but I think some of that has definitely gone away. It's not as intense today as it was at that time." However, when it comes to interviewing athletes with gigantic egos, "Human nature doesn't change that much," says Anne.

One of her favorite memories of ego management involves

Reggie Jackson of the New York Yankees. "Hall of Famer, a great, great baseball player. He's your classic example of a really big ego. You don't get a much bigger ego than Reggie Jackson. When I was working in sports, he was at the peak of his career. It was extremely difficult for any journalist to interview him. To Reggie Jackson, journalists were like little mosquitoes biting an elephant. He didn't like them. He didn't need the visibility. He was sick and tired of the same questions."

Whenever the Yankees came to Detroit, the dilemma for sportscasters was how to get an interview with Jackson, the biggest star on the team. "For me as a new, young, first-ever woman in the sports department, what were they going to do to test me? They were going to say, 'Okay, Anne, you go down to Tiger Stadium and get an interview with Reggie Jackson.' So I took this on as a challenge. I did my homework first; I did a whole lot of research. I thought really hard ahead of time about what I could ask him that would be interesting to him and would appeal to his ego."

An hour or two before every game, when both teams were taking warm-up batting practice, journalists were given access to the ballplayers. "They were out on the field before the fans were there, and journalists were allowed to approach them and ask for an interview. They didn't have to respond, but you could ask," says Anne.

On the day of the Yankees game, Anne went out to the field to find Jackson. "He was standing at the back, where they have a big batting cage set up behind the plate for when they're practicing. There were other journalists hanging around waiting to talk to players. Reggie Jackson was actually, I would call it, *posed.* He was standing directly behind the plate. There was another player inside the batting cage swinging at the pitches, and Reggie had his arm leaning almost at eye level on the bar that wraps around the batting cage, and he was just watching the pitches come across the plate. Nobody was anywhere near him; no one would bother him. So I walked up to him, and I knew that the other reporters were kind of laughing: 'Watch this one. Wait till you see what happens here.'

"I walked up to him until I was standing beside him. He was looking straight ahead. I said, 'Reggie, my name is Anne Doyle. I'm a reporter. Could I talk to you for a minute?' Well, he never even turned. He never looked at me. He never acknowledged that I was there. He didn't turn his head. He didn't do anything. So then I said to him, *'Señor Jackson, mi nombre es Anne Doyle. Estaba pensando si podria hablar con usted en Español un poco?'* He shifted his eyes toward me. He still didn't move his head.

"I knew that he spoke Spanish, and luckily I did too. Most people didn't know that about him, but in my research I had found out that his maternal grandmother was Castilian and spoke fluent Spanish, and that he was starting to help other Latin players who were coming into baseball at that time and didn't speak English. What I had said to him was, 'Mr. Jackson, my name is Anne Doyle. I'm wondering if I could talk to you a little in Spanish.'

"I asked the question again. Finally he turned his whole body around toward me and said, *'Absolutamente.'* And the other journalists were just standing there like, 'How the hell did she get Reggie Jackson to do an interview with her?' I got an exclusive, which we broadcast in Spanish with English subtitles."

Anne is very clear on the reasons her approach worked. "It was understanding that, okay, he had a big, big ego, but what was his need? What was it that I could do to showcase him? And it was a win-win for both us. I got the interview, and he got *not* to talk to some little punk reporter in another town about the same old questions he gets asked all the time. Instead, I asked him about Latin players coming into the league."

A seasoned news reporter before she went into sports, Anne had already learned a few lessons about soothing big egos. "You don't wing it with somebody like Reggie Jackson. When you're dealing with someone who's a big ego, you say, 'Let me think here. How am I going to break through and connect with this person?'" And Anne mentions a power we'll return to often in this book: recognizing the other person's reality. "Your reality is *I need an interview with Reggie Jackson.* His reality is *I could give a rat's ass about doing another interview with some idiot reporter.* So it's all about them. I had to find something that would be intriguing to Reggie Jackson, and I had to give him a chance to showcase something special about himself."

POWER #4

Manage Opposition by Giving It Nothing to Oppose

In any persuasion campaign, there will be people who are with you, people who are against you, and undecideds. Sometimes the ones who are against you will forcefully attack you or your position. In those cases, the best response is usually to give the opposition nothing to oppose. It's the same principle that some Eastern martial arts techniques, such as aikido, are based on.

When you're debating somebody, it's never a matter of good versus evil. However, it's instructive to know how Buddhists view that cosmic conflict. Buddhism holds that evil will always divide itself. It's like the ego. The ego will keep separating itself from every other ego by wanting more. Whether it's cars or houses or money or women or recognition or stardom or any of those things, it will constantly try. Evil, too, is constantly trying to divide. It doesn't have any choice but to divide. When somebody is really on the wrong side—an extreme example would be a crime organization—they'll eventually begin to fight among themselves because, according to Buddhism, there are always alternate agendas and egos in evil that continually want to split.

Goodness, on the other hand, will always try to come together and unite. In everyday power struggles, you will always be in a stronger position if you are seen as the person who wants to bring the room together, even when someone is attacking you.

Managing opposition by giving it nothing to oppose simply means don't fight back. The strategy plays out in slightly different ways depending on the situation. If it's just you and one other person having an argument, the natural tendency is to respond to every attack. Next time, instead of responding, silently nod as if you see the other person's point and just let it sit. Give it a few minutes. In my experience, 90 percent of the time the other person will moderate his or her own position. All things tend toward balance, and people innately know when they've crossed the line. If they don't moderate themselves, chances are they have bigger issues and you won't resolve them in one argument anyway. But when you trust the person you're talking to and they cross the line a little bit, they'll know it, and not opposing them allows room for their anger to die down.

In group situations, a similar approach is possible. In Power #3, I advised you not to respond to a big ego who is trying to dominate the room. If you are perceiving that person as petty and insecure, chances are everyone else is too. In the same way, if someone launches an attack on your idea in a group setting, often you can sit back and not respond at all while the person's words hang in the air and the rest of the group comes to their own conclusions. Then you can go back to the original goal without making a value judgment about the person. That reinforces you as the leader and uniter, and it subtly puts the opponent in his or her place without your having to say anything.

If ignoring a challenge doesn't end the opposition, you can manage it by redirecting the energy. In focus groups I sometimes encounter a participant who's feeling belligerent or who gets stuck on a point and wants to keep butting heads with me. In those cases, the most effective move is to start agreeing with the person or acknowledging his or her point of view. When I do, the person's opposition has nowhere to go. Once the knee-jerk opposition subsides, I can come back and approach the topic from a different angle. I'm not capitulating about my main position, but I know that everything is a matter of degree. In a focus group or any group debate, arguments usually turn into subarguments. Without losing any important ground you can say, "I see your point," and leave it at that. Or you can rephrase the other person's point and ask, "So is that what you're saying?" The other person will respond, "That's right." You can then say, "Well, that's interesting," and now you're done.

Managing opposition when you are not part of the argument calls for a different approach. If everyone is in an equal position of power, what often happens is that when someone makes a suggestion and another person opposes it, the first person will immediately dig in his or her heels. If you're witnessing this, it's a good opportunity to remind everyone of the goal—"Why are we here today?" In doing that you'll reassert your leadership role and give the two adversaries a chance to back off while still retaining face.

In group situations where there is a clear superior, I've noticed that strong leaders will sometimes allow heated arguments to take place, trusting that the group will resolve the problem on its own. Experienced CEOs know that if they immediately step in on the debate, all they're doing is limiting creativity and imposing their will. So they're patient and allow the room to work things through. The best CEOs seem to intuitively know when to sit back and when to guide the debate. Sometimes they'll let it go on for an hour and a half, and when the group finally makes a decision, they'll just say, "I think that's a great idea. Let's go." They won't take credit for it, or say, "Hey, remember? That was my idea in the first place." Because now the group owns the idea. Other times, if the debate is starting to head in the wrong direction, the CEO will ask questions to steer the debate in a productive direction, knowing that eventually the group will come to the right conclusion.

Whether you are among equals or in the leadership role, the main concept to remember about opposition is that you can't swim against the current—you won't get anywhere. You've got to swim with the current and redirect it. To do that, you're letting silence work for you. You're finding common ground with your opponent. And you're always going back to the goal that the group is trying to accomplish together.

POWER #5

Make Your Weakness Your Strength

We all have our weaknesses, and when our goal is to persuade, we need to turn those weaknesses into strengths. Equally important, we need to speak up about them. In most business settings, where persuasion is personal and takes place between two people or within a small group, a trait that is perceived by others as a weakness—or that you personally experience as a weakness—may need to be acknowledged out loud by you. That way, you can control people's perception of the weakness and recast it as a strength.

In politics, candidates are forced to turn their weaknesses

into strengths in a very public way. The most famous example is probably Ronald Reagan's quip during a debate with Walter Mondale in 1984. Reagan, who was seventy-three at the time, announced, "I will not make age an issue of this campaign. I am not going to exploit, for political purposes, my opponent's youth and inexperience."

The weakness-into-strength positioning begins at the moment a political career is launched, when the first-time candidate is accused of being inexperienced. The standard response is "That's right! I *am* an outsider, and I'll be a breath of fresh air in the stale, corrupt halls of power." In the 2008 Democratic primaries, Barack Obama famously ran on his outsider status against longtime Washington insiders such as Hillary Clinton, Joe Biden, and Bill Richardson.

Obama's eventual opponent, John McCain, had a different weakness to contend with in the Republican primaries. Despite the fact that McCain had been a U.S. senator for twenty-two years, he was more widely known for having been a prisoner of war, as I discovered while focus-grouping conservative voters in South Carolina and Iowa. Rudolph Giuliani, the Republican front-runner at the time, was known for "leadership," a more positive trait when you're hoping to be president. McCain's campaign turned his weakness into a strength by concluding his television ads with the words,

"John McCain for Commander in Chief," rather than the standard "John McCain for President." It emphasized his potential for leadership as well as his military heroism, and helped to shift voters' perceptions about the traits a president should possess.

One of the most effective examples I've seen of turning a candidate's weakness into a strength was a mailer created by my former boss, Ray McNally, for George H. W. Bush during his 1988 campaign. Bush was accused in the primary of being too passive and unwilling to confront his rivals during debates or in the press. He had been a navy combat pilot in World War II, and Ray's piece featured a photo of Bush in a flight jacket standing on an aircraft carrier, along with a quote from one of Bush's speeches: "I am a quiet man, but I hear the quiet people others don't. The ones who raise the family, pay the taxes, meet the mortgage. I hear them and I am moved, and their concerns are mine."[1]

Arnold Schwarzenegger employed many weakness-to-strength tactics when he ran for governor of California, his first-ever public office. No experience in politics? He was not only an outsider but an outsider with his own fortune, which made him especially "incorruptible." Too accustomed to being the boss, not used to the give-and-take of the state legislature?

Well, that was what the dysfunctional California state government needed, a take-charge guy. Arnold has been turning his weaknesses into strengths all his life. Not long after he arrived in the United States, he and a friend decided to start a bricklaying business. Arnold's heavy Austrian accent was a weakness, in that it was sometimes difficult for potential customers to understand him. So he advertised his services as "Austrian bricklaying," increased his prices, and instantly became a European artisan rather than a foreigner with an accent.

Which brings us to an interesting question: What is a weakness? Things such as gender, race, an accent, height, and so forth are often experienced as disadvantages in the workplace, even though they aren't weaknesses in the same sense that, for example, a stutter or dyslexia or extreme shyness is. Because of that, I almost decided to call this chapter "Turn Your Differences into Strengths." But in addition to sounding way too politically correct, that misses the point. If it feels like a weakness to you in the situation where you want to be persuasive, you need to get it out on the table and turn it into a strength.

For instance, women clearly are not weaker than men in the business world. But if you're the only woman in a room full of male colleagues, there's a chance you might feel at a disadvantage. If so, gender could feel like a weakness to you within that room. In my business, where we often deal with medical insurance issues that focus on female patients, being a woman is definitely an advantage. And it's not just my business, it's any business. If you're selling copiers, it's likely that at least half the people making copies are women. In most sales situations half the audience is going to be women. So if you're part of a team that has anything to do with marketing to the general public, being female is a benefit.

I've seen women handle the disadvantage of being the only female in a room full of men by owning that perspective instead of ignoring it. It can be as simple as saying something like, "Can I tell you what I'm hearing from the women? Because they account for 43 percent of this market." This doesn't imply that you *only* know about the female market. It signals that you have access to information that the men may not, and that you are confident enough to share it. The same thing goes for anyone who is a minority in a specific group.

Half the battle is internal. It's understanding that you're as good as everyone else, and believing that what you may perceive as a weakness is actually a strength. The Buddhists teach that the thought is the root, and the root becomes the tree. This is true no matter what your personal profile. Believe that your "weakness" is a strength, and you will soon see it in that light. It isn't a matter of fooling yourself, it's a matter of being open to a different perspective.

Young people or people of any age who are transitioning to a different career often have to contend with the "lack of experience" weakness. There are two ways you can combat that. First, understand that you are bringing a fresh perspective, which is valuable in any situation. Second, realize that everyone always has some type of experience to bring to the table. Your task is to make that experience relate to whatever it is you're doing. Let's say you're interviewing for a job selling an Internet service. Maybe you can honestly say, "I've been talking about the benefits of this type of service ever since I heard about it three years ago." Just because you haven't been in that profession doesn't mean you don't bring a viewpoint and some experience, either as an enthusiastic observer or as a consumer.

There are very few weaknesses that cannot be turned into strengths. The formula is to think about what effect your weakness has on the way you interact with the world, to identify the positives in that, and to tell others about it. Looking no further than my own staff, I can give you a good example. I hired Jeff several years ago because he was a hard worker, incredibly organized, had excellent analytic skills, and was a really funny, friendly person. After working with him for a few weeks, I noticed that he occasionally seemed to miss a word or phrase I was saying. No big deal, but it distracted me and aroused my curiosity. In a persuasion situation, that would not be good. He was a young guy, in his late twenties, so I was surprised when he eventually told me that he had a 40 percent hearing loss.

"I think you ought to be very up front with people about it," I said. He decided to take my advice. These days, within a few minutes of being introduced to someone, Jeff will say, "I have a 40 percent hearing loss; would you mind sitting close to me so I can hear you?" Later, at an appropriate moment, he'll tell them, "You know, one thing about this hearing loss is that I've become a pro at reading body language. It's really useful when we're doing focus groups. I can read lips pretty well too." People are always intrigued by the lip-reading—it's an excellent conversation starter.

What about personality traits such as shyness or being a tad loud and opinionated? These, too, can be turned into strengths when they are openly acknowledged by you: "I'm really passionate about my ideas, and sometimes I might get a bit *too* passionate, so let me know if I'm doing that." Or if you're shy: "I've been quiet so far because I've been listening very carefully to what everyone's saying. So can I tell you what

I'm hearing?" That will definitely make the others stop and pay attention.

Some of the nation's most successful CEOs have had to wrestle with weaknesses in the form of learning disabilities. A 2003 *New York Times* article about such CEOs included people like John Chambers of Cisco Systems, Richard Branson of the Virgin Group, and Charles Schwab of the investment firm that bears his name. Schwab explained that although he always excelled at math, reading was and remains difficult for him. As a result of his dyslexia, he developed a different way of viewing the world. He told the *Times*, "I've frustrated some of my associates because I could see the end zone of a particular thing quicker than they could, so I was moving ahead to conclusions. . . . I go straight from step A to Z and say: This is the outcome. I can see it."

Kinko's founder Paul Orfalea struggled with dyslexia and attention deficit disorder. Too antsy to sit still for meetings, he decided instead to travel to various Kinko's locations and observe what worked and what didn't: "Every location, there was something there that every store could learn from. So I was going store to store, looking for gold." A learning disorders expert interviewed for the *Times* article explained that dyslexia had made some of these high-achieving executives particularly adaptable and resilient, and that the condition naturally led them to think outside the box. The CEOs themselves believe that their disabilities have given them "a heightened sense of empathy."[2]

In any job, making your weakness your strength is a positive. But when you're persuading, it's important to remember the other half of the equation: talking about it out loud, so that the unacknowledged "weakness" doesn't distract people from your message.

POWER #6

Find One Thing to Like About Everyone in the Room

In any type of persuasion, your listeners have to believe in *you* as much as your message. If they don't like you, they won't believe in you. Luckily, getting other people to like you is easy—they'll like you if you like them. So you've got to find at least one thing to like about everyone in the room.

A sales trip I took nearly a decade ago proved to me how important this is. I had traveled from California to New York with a couple of colleagues to make my first big East Coast pitch for Jury Impact. I was sure that many of the strategies I had developed in marketing and politics would also work in the courtroom. Jurors were listening to a story, the same way voters did when they listened to a politician or consumers did when they watched a commercial. Why not teach trial lawyers how to fine-tune their story like marketers and politicians, and then deliver it in words jurors could understand instead of legalese that put them to sleep?

I was thirty-two, pitching to a room full of fifty-year-old trial lawyers at the top of their game. The jury consultants they usually hired came from established companies and had PhDs in psychology. I was younger than everyone in the room, we were advocating a fundamentally different approach to jury consulting, we were a start-up firm, and to top it all off we were from Southern California.

The meeting took place on the thirty-eighth floor of a Manhattan office tower. Seated around an enormous conference table, with an eye-popping city view looming behind them, the attorneys listened to our pitch. They seemed a little surprised by our concept and were mildly intrigued. The meeting went all right, but only all right. Afterward, as my colleagues and I were riding the elevator down, one of them said, "The third guy on the left was unbelievably arrogant, wasn't he? The whole bunch of them were old and stuck in their ways. They haven't had a new idea in fifteen years."

I suddenly realized why the meeting had fizzled. We needed to go in there liking these men and women. Otherwise, they were going to sense our dislike and it would kill the sale. The attorneys were seasoned and successful; there had to be a way we could get them to understand that we were offering something new and different, a valuable edge over their competition.

"They're smart. I'm sure they'll get it," I told my colleagues. I thought about Danny, another member of our fledgling firm who had yet to close a single deal. He didn't like the people he was pitching to, I realized. He always had something negative to say about them after he left the room, but that was really a reflection of Danny and how he viewed the world, not a reflection of them.

The next time we pitched to a group of attorneys, we changed our expectations. Instead of arrogant and rigid, we assumed they would be shrewd, experienced professionals who would recognize the innovation we brought to the table. When we had those expectations, we found the attorneys to be much more enthusiastic. That's how we played it from then on, and ten years down the road I have to say it's worked out well for us.

In Buddhism, the sin is not the action; the sin is the thought, because the action can only follow the thought. I've found that just thinking to myself, "I like those people," changes the way I feel about them. I get this smile on my face, and (with some exceptions) all of a sudden everyone tends to like me. I do realize that when you walk into a room, you're going to have a gut reaction to certain individuals, and sometimes it's going to be negative. But gut reactions aren't always valid. Often they're just a reflection of your own insecurity or ambivalence. To resist negative first impressions, I encourage my team to do a "mind-flip." Every trait can be viewed two ways, so when you flip negative to positive:

Stubborn becomes resolute.
Skeptical becomes careful.
Silent becomes thoughtful.
Critical becomes analytical.
Aggressive becomes passionate.

Working with attorneys has taught me how valuable the mind-flip is. In my business, we're often brought in by a corporate client to assist a legal team that isn't always thrilled about us being "forced" on them. One trial lawyer called me and demanded, "Why do I need you guys?" Everybody had warned me he was difficult (actually, they used the word *asshole*). But I thought, "This guy's straightforward. I can appreciate that." Three years later, he's quoted on our website saying I'm one of the best message consultants in America. If I had thought of his approach as abrasive, I'll bet he wouldn't have liked me either. But because I honestly saw it as straightforward, we now get along and enjoy a mutually prosperous relationship.

The find-something-to-like approach works everywhere, not just in business settings. A friend of mine used it to defuse a situation at her son's middle school. Her eighth grader, Luke, had been complaining about the vice principal, a big, brusque, bald-headed guy who patrolled the yard at lunchtime. Luke said the VP had been picking on him and had decided he was a troublemaker. Naturally, Luke was innocent, just like every other eighth-grade boy who walks the planet. The VP was a jerk. "He's got some cool ties, though," Luke reported.

A few weeks later at Back-to-School Night, Luke's mom saw the VP in the cafeteria. His splashy tie featured tropical fish. "My son loves your ties," she commented in passing. The man lit up like a Christmas tree. "He talked for five minutes about his hundreds of ties, how he's collected them from all over the world. It was sort of endearing," she told me. "I'm hoping the next time he sees my son, he'll remember that Luke likes his ties." A key point is that the tie compliment was true—Luke really did like them. When she told Luke about the conversation, it made her son like the VP a little bit more too, and he stopped complaining about being hassled at lunchtime.

Sometimes you may need to look very closely to find a likeable trait. I've learned to like someone's smile, or his demeanor, or her joke. I've learned to lighten up, and if all else fails, to see the beauty in the situation and remember that everyone has a family and everyone just wants to be liked.

POWER #7

Use the First Five Minutes to Make People Feel Safe

When your main goal is to persuade, the first five minutes are not so much about impressing other people as they are about putting them at ease. People's egos are on high alert the first few minutes of a meeting, and you want to relax them so they'll be receptive to your ideas. Before I share some tactics for making people feel safe, the standard advice about first impressions is worth repeating: smile, make eye contact, and offer a firm (not bone-crushing) handshake.

I'd like to pass along three other etiquette tips as well. The first one is very basic. If someone asks how you are, don't just say, "Fine." Say, "Fine, thank you. How are you?" I know it seems obvious, but people forget to do this all the time, and it sends a subtle negative message that you're self-absorbed, rude, or both.

The second tip is for women: Use your last name. I can't tell you how often I've been in business meetings where we're all asked to introduce ourselves and the women say, "I'm Kathy," or "I'm Susan," as if they're at the gym rather than in a conference room. You'll never hear a group of businessmen introduce themselves with "I'm Bill," "I'm Kevin," "I'm Greg." It's just not going to happen. Business is still largely a man's world, and using your full name signals that you're comfortable in it.

Finally, if you're a visitor and someone asks if you'd like something to drink, request water and be sure to thank them when they hand it to you. People want to do something nice for you, but not too much. This is a surefire way to make them feel good about themselves without inconveniencing them. It's more effective than saying, "I don't need anything, thanks."

Google and social networking sites like Facebook add a layer of information to your meeting that you've got to take into account. If it's the first time you're meeting the group, look up the principals so you're up-to-date on their backgrounds and recent activities. You can bring the topic up yourself during the first five minutes—"I looked you up online; you've got quite a résumé"—or mention it when they start talking about something you recognize from your research. It shows that you've done your homework. It goes without saying that you should also visit their company's website.

As for Facebook, if the people you're meeting with have Facebook pages with open access, you're in luck. Check them out. More to the point, what's on *your* Facebook page? Assume that whoever you're meeting has read it. At my firm we Facebook everyone we interview, be they job candidates, possible clients, or potential jurors. We were all set to interview one young guy for a position when we saw that he had written on his Facebook page, "Every girl's got a little slut in her." Not too smart, considering (a) it's offensive, and (b) the people who would have been interviewing him were women.

If you already know the people you're meeting with, use the first five minutes to make them feel valued. If it's a superior, acknowledge that the person is taking time out of his or her busy day. There are a couple of ways to do this. You can just say it: "Thanks for meeting with me. I know you're busy." You can be more specific, for instance by asking about a project the person is working on. Or you can be bolder and really make an impression. Think about the last time this superior complained about something—babies crying on the airplane or the restaurant that never puts enough mayo on a sandwich. When you go in to meet with the person, bring a pair of inexpensive headphones or a jar of mayo, set it on the desk, and say, "I've solved your problem. Can I have a minute of your time?" It's using a light touch to signal that you listen to the other person and care enough to actually go out and buy the item.

I've had people do this with me, and I get a big kick out of it. Once, when I was at a rather stuffy restaurant with eight colleagues, I asked one of them how her wine tasted. She replied, "It has a hint of gooseberry." That cracked me up, and I gave her the hardest time about it for the next two hours. I was eating my steak—"Mmmm. Gooseberry." My rolls—"Gooseberry!" A month later, I got a gift basket of gooseberry jelly in the mail from this woman. I thought to myself, "If she ever needs anything, I'm going to give it to her." It was a brilliant (and very nice) gesture.

During the first five minutes you'll be making a visual impact as well as a verbal one. The conventional wisdom is to match your style of dress to that of the people you'll be meeting. I agree, but only up to a point. When you're selling a service, you may not want to look exactly like the folks you're persuading. If you're just like them, why do they need you? For example, most of the people I work with are executives or attorneys. Why would I want to dress in a dark conservative business suit like they do? They don't need another lawyer, they need a guy who can contribute something new. By dressing differently, I not only set myself apart, I also signal that I'm not competing with them, which makes them feel safe. The clothing I wear to these meetings is casual yet classy, maybe a pullover sweater and jeans, both of which are obviously expensive. It's an old but true dictum of salesmanship that if you're going to sell something valuable, you need to look affluent.

At focus groups I choose slightly different clothing, usually jeans and a pink shirt. In these situations, when I need to connect with people quickly, I can use the shirt as an icebreaker. I'll say something like, "My wife just bought this shirt for me and I'm a little uncomfortable in pink. On a scale of one to ten, ten being the best shirt, one being the worst, what would you give it?" Someone will say, "Ten," and a few folks will nod, and then someone else will say, "Two," and I'll come back with, "My face or my shirt?" It's a little corny, it's self-deprecating, but now they're engaged. It opens people up. The number scale gives them a sense of control, which (you guessed it) makes them feel safe. For purposes of running a focus group, that's exactly what I want.

By the way, other people will notice and be curious about

whatever you're carrying. I'm always fascinated by the paraphernalia of the different groups I deal with. Attorneys pride themselves on hauling around suitcase-size briefcases loaded with all their documents. It's the opposite with politicians, who are told never to bring a briefcase into a room. Pay attention the next time you see a politician on TV—they're always empty-handed. Their assistant has the briefcase. The politician is sending the message, "I'm not here to take notes for you. I'm not a bookworm or a wonk; I'm a confident, charismatic leader." They've thought about how their look will be perceived, and so should everyone.

POWER #8

Stay in the Present

There's nothing worse for a person's ego than trying to talk to you while you're checking your BlackBerry—except maybe having to stop mid-sentence while you answer your cell phone or text someone. These devices should be turned off when you meet with people you want to persuade. It doesn't matter what everyone else is doing; if you're the only person not checking your BlackBerry, that's okay. You will be the only one entirely in the present. You'll notice more about the others, and the people you're talking with will have a positive impression of you even if they've been checking *their* BlackBerrys like fiends.

All great communicators excel at staying in the moment, especially politicians. Years ago, a friend told me about meeting Margaret Thatcher, the former prime minister of Great Britain. Mrs. Thatcher is not someone you would normally think of as warm and fuzzy, but she was a tremendously successful politician. My friend was in a greeting line at an event she was attending, and he couldn't stop talking about how charismatic she was. Naturally I asked for details. He said, "She took my hand with both of hers, made eye contact, and asked me how I was. We had about a fifteen-second conversation, but I'll remember it the rest of my life because she was completely engaged in what I was saying."

It's not hard to learn the moves: eye contact, press some flesh, ask a question about the other person. What's difficult is *not* paying attention to the dozens of distractions all around you, and treating every one of the hundreds of people you meet to that same level of attention and interest.

Once I visited my Buddhist teacher, Master Truong, after not having seen him for a long while. There was hardly any furniture in his house, so we sat cross-legged on the living room floor. I was telling him what I had been up to, and a few minutes into the conversation I noticed an ant walking up his neck. It walked along his cheek, and then it walked on his forehead, and then down his nose. I said, "Master Truong, you have an ant on your nose," and then leaned in to brush it off. He stopped me and said, "I know. It's not bothering anyone." He was aware of everything, but he was paying attention to me alone, watching my every movement, listening and not casting judgments, making me feel valued. It gave me a deep sense of peace, and that's the feeling I hope to give other people, at least a little bit, when I give them my full attention.

Another Buddhist monk, the Dalai Lama, is famous for being entirely in the present when he meets with visitors, which he has done thousands of times. The following excerpt, from the book *Living Tibet: The Dalai Lama in Dharamsala* by Nanci Rose, is one of the best descriptions I've read about the experience:

> His Holiness the Dalai Lama waits to greet you on the sidewalk. Bowing slightly and beaming broadly, he is thoroughly happy to see you, as though finally reuniting with a dear and long-lost special friend. . . .
>
> In the simply furnished meeting room adorned with a few Tibetan Buddhist paintings, you wonder how this session should begin. The Dalai Lama waits. Gradually it dawns on you that it is up to you alone to set the tone. In fact, His Holiness seems to absorb the mood, responding at each moment to your own state of mind. If you have

> philosophic or mystical questions, His Holiness aligns himself as closely as possible with the tradition or experience from which you speak. If your focus highlights political or social concerns, his responses mirror your framework. . . . Regardless of the topic, brief words of practical advice and grounded viewpoint are woven into a conversation that begins and ends with your own initiative. . . . He is simply there for you, to become engaged in a warm, personal exchange.

The power of being in the present is one that great spiritual masters attain, and we can all benefit from attempting it in our own way. It begins by turning off the BlackBerry or iPhone, looking the other person in the eye, and listening.

POWER #9

Recognize Their Reality

I've conducted focus groups from Nashua, New Hampshire, to San Diego, California, and most places in between, and one thing is clear to me: The number of different personal realities is infinite. Understanding that is fundamental to successful persuasion, because it is always easiest to convince people of what they already believe. Every word you speak travels through the filter of your listener's personal experiences, and the opinions that emerge are shaped by those experiences. The challenge in persuasion is to recognize your audience's reality, align it with yours, and then create a common benefit that is your goal.

When we work with attorneys, we tell them, "Never argue against a jury's predispositions. You won't win." If we focus-group a case and explore every juror predisposition, and we can't find any that fit with our lawyers' argument, we advise them to settle out of court. But if we uncover predispositions that will let the lawyers talk about a case in a way that gets jurors thinking, "I remember that in my own life," it changes the whole ball game. That's why one of the most effective things you can say to a jury is, "Remember when . . . ?" If you seize upon experiences your jurors can personally relate to, the rest of your story will seem more true, including things they have *not* experienced.

In everyday life you don't focus-group the people you want to persuade, but you can recognize their reality and play to their predispositions using the same tactics I use. Let's say you're a supervisor and your goal is to switch computer platforms from Mac to PC. You might think you already know what your employees believe—"Macs rule. We don't want to change." But to really understand their point of view, you need to dig deeper. You can introduce the subject with "Remember when . . ." the way lawyers do: "Remember when we first launched this company and had a choice between Macs and PCs? We chose Macs because they were the most advanced graphic arts platform. They're still great." You're stating the obvious to establish a personal experience that you share with them. Now you can transition to your goal: "PCs have evolved since then, and I'm considering switching platforms so that we're more compatible with other companies. I'd like to get some feedback from you about it."

Now you can listen to your audience. A good strategy is to go around the room and ask what each person has heard other people say about PCs. You're essentially giving them all permission to express their fears. Take notes, and in your own words repeat back what you heard them say. The tactic is called active listening, and it's a way to demonstrate that you hear people and care about their concerns. Equally important, now you know what their objections will be.

The typical Mac-user perception of PCs is that the software has glitches and PCs attract more viruses than Macs do. How do you align that reality with your goal? First, acknowledge an aspect that is true: PCs do attract more viruses. You'll probably always need to devote more effort to virus protection with PCs than you would with Macs. Next, offer an explanation: PCs get more viruses because more people use PCs than use Macs. Then transition to a positive about this same truth: Because so many more companies use PCs, switching platforms will make interaction with most other companies much smoother. Clients will be happier, and that should improve working conditions for everyone.

Note the progression: It begins with agreeing that PCs do get more viruses. You have not argued, "They don't get that many viruses! It doesn't matter anyway because our virus protection is the best." *You are looking for something you can agree about.* The point is not to disprove their reality but to understand and acknowledge it. You want to agree with them and unite to achieve a common goal—in this case, new computers that will make everyone's job easier.

It may not be possible to address every one of their complaints this way, but it's also not necessary. Like a trial lawyer, you're opening a door. You're making your audience receptive to your plan by acknowledging their reality so they'll trust your judgment. When they actually get the PCs on their desks, they'll be able to see the advantages and some of their concerns will fade away.

If you're the boss, there's always the unspoken reality that your employees have no choice except to do what you ask them to do. A little humor can help you acknowledge that reality. For instance, I tend to use the term *we* a lot. So in a meeting with my team I'll say, "We have to do six rounds of docs this month. And when I say 'we,' you do know that I really mean *you*, right?" They laugh because they know they're the ones who will end up doing the work, but at least I recognize it.

When you're pitching a service or product, you can acknowledge that you are one of many: "I know you get a lot of people coming to you with ideas. I appreciate your hearing me out on this one." Or "I know you have to make a lot of difficult budget decisions. I think this might be really cost-effective for you." The words I use to soothe the egos of lawyers and CEOs serve double duty by also recognizing their reality: "You're the one who's sticking your neck out here. I get to come in and give advice, and I get to take credit whether you win or lose." Or if I'm talking to an ally in any situation: "I know you're putting your credibility on the line by backing me on this." That is their perception of the situation—it's their reality—and my recognizing it makes them more willing to trust me and take my side.

Reality Check: Can a Baseball Team Be from Two Cities?

The Angels baseball team has a long history in Southern California, and just like a starlet or a rapper, its name has changed a few times along the way. When it was founded by Gene Autry in 1961, it was the Los Angeles Angels. In 1966 it moved twenty-five miles south to Anaheim, in Orange County, and became the California Angels. The Walt Disney Company bought the team in 1996 and renamed it the Anaheim Angels. In 2003 the team changed hands again. The new owner wanted to expand the Angels' appeal to a greater area of Southern California, so he changed the name to the Los Angeles Angels of Anaheim. And all hell broke loose.

"It's geographically confusing and absurd," fumed Anaheim city spokesman John Nicoletti. "No other professional sports franchise that I know of has two different cities in its name." The city of Anaheim filed a breach-of-contract lawsuit against the owner, saying that the name change violated the spirit of the lease between Anaheim and the Angels.

Why the outrage? It's physically impossible for one team to be from two cities, so the name violated everyone's reality and sounded laughable. Making matters worse was the fact that people who live in Orange County aren't very fond of Los Angeles, and vice versa. Although Orange and Los Angeles counties are right next door to each other, the residents see themselves as inhabiting separate worlds. Those living "behind the Orange Curtain" consider L.A. a chaotic mess populated by criminals and limousine liberals, while Angelinos think the O.C. is full of SUV-driving Republicans, chain restaurants, and mini-malls. People in Orange County adamantly believe that it is completely different from L.A. That is their reality. I learned the depth of their belief when we were hired by the new owner's legal team to help them fight the city of Anaheim's lawsuit.

Our plan was to first conduct surveys of people in Orange County to assess their feelings about the name change. We found that a stunning 80 percent thought the Angels had violated the spirit of their contract with the city and that the team should be forced to change their name back to Anaheim Angels. The new owner's contention that Orange County and Los Angeles were one media market particularly irked them. They indignantly pointed out that Orange County had its own newspapers and radio and television stations.

While we were researching, tensions were mounting. Entrepreneurial fans were cashing in on the community's anger by selling T-shirts and other items emblazoned with slogans such as "We are not L.A." and "Anaheim Angels of Anaheim." Capitalizing on the furor, California State Assemblyman Tom Umberg introduced a "Truth in Sports Advertising Act," which would have required the team to state on all their tickets and merchandise that the home of the Angels was Anaheim, not Los Angeles. The media kept stoking the story, and people in the O.C. kept seething. It was an atmosphere ripe for jury nullification, when emotions tempt jurors to vote according to their feelings and neglect the law.

During the focus groups, it became clear that denying the jurors' reality would lose us the lawsuit. As we put it in our report to the legal team, "Don't fight the predisposition that Orange County is separate from Los Angeles—constantly remind jurors that this case isn't about feelings toward L.A., it's about a contract. . . . We don't believe it will be possible to completely overcome the natural dislike of the 'Los Angeles' name by Orange County residents. However, by acknowledging the natural desire to make this about 'community pride,' the defense can then ask the jury to remember that this case is really about interpreting a contract."

The lawyers' task was to acknowledge the jurors' reality and then pivot to one of the big three concepts—choice, fairness, or accountability—that you will read about in Power #10. In this case, it was all about the fairness of honoring a contract. The city of Anaheim had signed the 1996 contract with Disney, the Angels' previous owner, fully understanding that the team's name might change. In fact, they had tried to insist that the name remain the Anaheim Angels to the exclusion of anything else, but Disney refused. The city signed anyway. It wouldn't be fair to let the city change the rules now.

The city of Anaheim's legal team argued that the spirit of the contract—the intent—was that the Anaheim Angels be the sole name. They were hoping an angry, emotional jury would agree with them. It might have worked if we had not already deflated the anger by acknowledging the jurors' reality. Our strategy prevailed. After the verdict, Juror Jack Clay explained the thought process of the majority of the jurors: "It's not so much whether we like it. It's whether [the new owner] had a right to do it. . . . Suppose there were no witnesses to give you any information on intent. Then what would you have? You'd have the contract."

Today, "Los Angeles Angels of Anaheim" is still the team's legal name, although you won't find it on their website or merchandise—just "Angels." And the last laugh has to go to the Long Beach Armada baseball team, located a few miles west of Anaheim. In 2007, they officially changed their name to the "Long Beach Armada of Los Angeles of California of the United States of North America Including Barrow, Alaska." Said team manager and ex-MLB all-star Darrell Evans, "Instead of burying our hometown at the back of our long name, we are proud to lead off with Long Beach at the top of the order. Just like in baseball, when you lead off with your best hitter."

POWER #10

Make It About Choice, Fairness, and Accountability

Choice, *fairness*, and *accountability* are three of the most popular words in the English language. Politicians learned this a long time ago, which is why the words pop up so often in political campaigns. There are the initiatives: "pro-choice" for reproductive rights, "controlled choice" for an anti-busing plan, "school choice" for school vouchers. There are the organizations: People for a Fair Deal . . . Fair Legal System . . . Fair Web . . . Fair Houston . . . and dozens more. And don't forget the countless legislative acts promising "accountability" in everything from contracting, to education, to presidential pardons.

The typical response to the words *choice, fairness*, or *accountability* is almost Pavlovian. It doesn't matter what the topic is, I can say, "I just want to make sure you have choices, and that in the end someone is held accountable so that we ensure the fairest result," and I'll get the whole room nodding in agreement. What does it mean? Something different to everyone. But the fact that they are all nodding is what's important, because from that point of agreement you can lead the discussion where you want it to go.

Let's take a closer look at each of these words in action. The surest bet is *choice*, because in our culture choice is seen as unquestionably good. We think of it as *free* choice, virtually synonymous with freedom. In the United States, the concept of individual freedom is just about next to godliness, so the word *choice* is particularly powerful.

Here's how we used choice recently in advising the legal team for an insurance company. As you probably know, the insurance industry is universally despised. Juries are inclined to decide against them and in favor of the little guy, even if the "little guy" is a group of sophisticated attorneys looking for a big payout. In this case, we were hired to conduct focus groups of potential jurors on behalf of one of America's largest health insurers. They were facing a class-action lawsuit involving a man who had been in a car accident. He went to a doctor for a series of physical therapy treatments, and the insurer paid the doctor's fee, about $100 a session. There was another doctor in town who charged $80, and the insurer had not made the man aware of this doctor. He was suing for the $20 difference, part of which he had to pay himself to meet the deductible. Expanded into a class-action lawsuit, it was $20 times thousands of other people who had not been made aware of less expensive doctors.

After explaining the basics of the case to our first focus group, we asked them, "Do you want insurance companies to choose your doctor for you?" Suddenly it was about choice. The man chose this particular doctor. The insurer didn't get involved in the choice. They paid a more expensive fee and now this guy wanted the difference. He could actually end up preventing the rest of us from having choices by forcing insurance companies to send us to the cheapest doctor.

This line of reasoning may sound obvious, but the case had been dragging on for seven years. It took a group of people who knew nothing about the situation—the people in our focus groups—to see it clearly. With our experience in simplifying cases and making them about choice, fairness, or accountability, we were able to narrow down the argument in about three hours during our first group. After that, I conducted more groups where I tried to nudge the jurors in the other direction to test the depth of their commitment to choosing their own doctor. But as soon as I delivered the sentence, "Don't you hate it when insurance companies try to choose your doctor for you?" I could not sway them, no matter how hard I tried. That's the power of choice.

When dealing with clients, offering a choice is an excellent way to present a plan. Naturally you should limit the choices—three is a good number—because you don't want to overwhelm them with so many options that it becomes frustrating. The three choices should all be ones you could live with. It's fine to tell your clients which option you prefer, all the while emphasizing that ultimately the choice is theirs. For example: "How do you want to handle this? I'm thinking we should run radio spots two weeks before the event. But we could also do a combination of radio and cable, or just cable. It's up to you." When I'm hired as a consultant I always say, "I work for you, so this is your decision. Here's my recommendation." Nine times out of ten, they take my advice.

Offering employees a choice is usually a wise move too. Unlike clients or customers, your staff has little power in their relationship with you. Anytime you're able to give them options—about anything from where to have the Christmas party to where to relocate—you're going to win their appreciation and a higher level of cooperation.

Fairness is a little trickier than choice because people's definition of what is fair varies according to their life circumstances. If you're for slavery reparations, your mind-set about fairness is going to be very different from that of someone who's never heard of it or is opposed to it. In the same way, your client's perception of fairness ("You should take my calls anytime, day or night") will be different than your spouse's. So when you use the word *fair*, you need to recognize that the other person's reality is not always the same as yours.

But regardless of each person's definition of fairness in a specific situation, everyone has a general sense of the concept. In fact, every argument my two little boys have is about whether or not something is fair. I see it in court all the time too: Amid the mind-numbing legal arguments, jurors listen for what is fundamentally fair. I remember a trial about a contract dispute where the lawyers droned on about the intricacies of the contract. Day after day, I watched the jurors' eyes glaze over. What they really wanted to know was how the twenty-eight-year-old assistant who was making a yearly salary of $36,000 went to $450,000 in three years. Turned out she was sleeping with the president. Unfair! It's nearly impossible to move people if they have become convinced of the basic unfairness of a situation. The O. J. Simpson trial is the ultimate example—decades of perceived unfairness at the hands of the Los Angeles Police Department led the jury to acquit O. J. Simpson in spite of overwhelming evidence that he was guilty.

How do you make fairness work for you? The most straightforward way is to say out loud that you want things to be fair. By inserting the word *fair* into the discussion, you're dignifying your listeners. You're boosting their egos by showing that you empathize with them, and that will make them more receptive to your ideas. You can simply say something like, "I want to make sure this plan is fair to everyone," or you can use words like *balance*: "It's important to me that in the end this is a balanced proposal." Opening with those statements lays a nice groundwork for becoming a leader, because everyone's thinking, "He wants to make sure we all succeed."

Accountability taps into the same emotional vein as fairness. It's especially powerful when you apply it to yourself, because then you can reasonably expect others to be accountable too. A good way to phrase it is with the words *checks and balances*: "Let's build in checks and balances, so that you're holding me accountable and we all ensure that we're successful." The checks and balances apply to the others too, whether they are clients or staff. The important point is that you go first. Then the others involved will have to either agree or explain why they don't want to be held accountable.

One of the most effective, if troubling, uses of accountability occurred during Michael Jackson's trial for child molestation. As we all learned, the King of Pop liked to share his bed with the young boys who stayed at his Neverland Ranch. The mother of one of the boys brought molestation charges against Jackson. To take the spotlight off the singer, his attorneys asked the jury what sort of mother would let her child sleep in a bed with a forty-year-old. Wasn't she responsible for that boy? Shouldn't she be held accountable? Jackson's lawyers needed a villain who wasn't Jackson, and they found her. In the jurors' minds, the bad mom who shirked her responsibility ended up seeming guiltier than Jackson.

Choice, fairness, and accountability are reliable default positions in any debate. One of my favorite tactics is to use them to stop an argument and turn it my way. No matter what the other person is saying, I can respond, "That's my point."

"What's your point?" the other person will ask.

"This is really about fairness [or choices, or making sure the right people are held accountable]."

It stops the conversation because the other person doesn't know where I'm going. But I do. I've taken them to the top of the food chain, so to speak: to the place where we agree, because everyone will always agree about choice, fairness, or accountability.

"Now let me explain how fairness fits into our idea of the best way to move forward."

I've redirected the debate by saying, "That's my point," and I've gotten everyone to listen. I've taken them all back to fairness, and I can take them all the way down the logic chain to the specific argument I want to make. If you argue correctly using choice, fairness, or accountability, you never lose.

POWER #11

Keep It Simple

A lawyer once told me, "I know I've got a good case if I can turn it into what I call cocktail talk. When I'm talking to my partner's spouse, can I boil the case down into a thirty-second argument that benefits me? If I can only boil it down into a thirty-second argument that benefits my opponent, I'm in trouble."

Attorneys, politicians, and marketers all know that repeating a brief, powerful message is crucial to winning. The side with the simplest story doesn't *always* prevail, but it always has a great advantage. Our whole jury consulting business is based on a situation that consistently occurs in corporate lawsuits: a suit is filed, and lawyers spend two years complicating it. We spend a few months boiling it back down to its essence so the lawyers can tell a simple story that plays to jurors' predispositions and convinces them of something they already believe. When the lawyers open their argument, they present it in thirty seconds. They then go on to say that in the coming days or weeks, they will prove their argument is true. If they don't have that thirty-second opening, their challenge will be much greater.

Whether it's persuading a group or selling a product, it's easiest to accomplish a goal if your story is simple. It's not because people are stupid—that's a mistake too many political strategists make. They think voters are dumb on both sides of the aisle, and they create dumb messages that insult the folks they're trying to persuade. People aren't dumb, they're inundated. We're all subjected to thousands of requests for our attention every day, from advertisements to piped-in music to television, iPods, and cell phones. You can't even take a ten-second ride in an elevator without having to stare at an ad on its wall. In self-defense, people have become selective about what they're willing to listen to. They are going to tune you out unless your story is simple, compelling, and most of all, relates to their personal experience.

I first learned about the power of a good story during my

years in marketing and political consulting, but it was my work with jurors that solidified my belief that this is true anytime, anywhere. In theory, jurors shouldn't even be interested in the simple version of a case. Their job is to listen carefully to every word of testimony, and they know it's a serious responsibility. Depending on the verdict, people could end up in jail or being awarded millions of dollars. Yet even the most conscientious jurors will find their attention flagging when confronted with complex testimony. Time and again I've seen them reduce thousands of pages of testimony to the simplest elements of a conflict. During one case, exit interviews revealed that the nuances of a high-stakes insurance lawsuit were pretty much irrelevant to the jurors. They found for the defense based on two simple facts: The plaintiff was able to choose his own doctor and he never paid anything out of his own pocket.

Your clients and colleagues are probably even less likely than jurors to pay close attention to a complicated story. As you go into details, they're going to be simplifying the story in their minds, spacing out, or jumping to conclusions. So to be effective at persuasion, you must tell a simple story that grabs their attention, makes them care, and gets them to unify behind your goal. In the workplace, creating a strong story is the best way not only to unify people but also to keep them focused and motivated. Your story is the engine that moves everyone forward.

You can shape an effective story after you have two pieces of knowledge: You need to be clear about what your goal is, and you need to understand your audience's reality. When you recognize their reality, you can align it with your goal, and then you can shape the story. For example, let's say you sell bottled water, and your goal is to sell two hundred thousand more bottles this year than last. Your audience in this case is consumers, people who drink water. To come up with the story that will achieve your goal, you have to think about your audience's reality. So you don't ask yourself, "How do we sell more water?" Instead, you ask yourself, "Why do people like water?" The answer is, "Water is essential to life." Your story, then, will have to be about why *your* water is essential to *their* life. Maybe something like, "Our water is the purest, safest water for your family," or, "Our water has extra vitamins to boost your health."

Those are advertising messages, obviously, but the same approach works anywhere. When creating your story, ask yourself, "What is my goal? What am I trying to accomplish? What's going to relate to my audience?"

For instance, my company's internal message statement is, "Our goal is to be the most sought-after message consultants in America." That allows me to be big or small, expensive or cheap; it creates a broad range of options for me but still motivates me and my team to go in one direction. Externally, my goal is to save clients money. My goal is to help them win the trial or the campaign. So if I'm hired as a trial consultant, in my first meeting with the legal team I'll announce, "My goal is to provide you with the messages that are going to help you relate to your audience and win that trial."

One situation where telling a simple, compelling story makes all the difference is when you're asking for a raise. As with any persuasion campaign, you want to start by bonding with the other person over a common goal. So your message would be: "I want to see all of us succeed. I want to be part of this company's future. I'm willing to make a long-term commitment." In this way you bond to your boss' reality, because he or she wants to succeed. Then you can tell your boss what you've done to support the company's goals, and what you plan to do in the future. Saying, "I work hard, can I have a raise?" is very different from saying, "We're in this together. I'm part of this team. Here are my plans to make this happen. Can I have a raise?" It changes the whole framework for how the boss will view your request.

A Sin for Every Story

From their origin in early Christian teachings through their present-day use in plots of major motion pictures, the seven deadly sins—lust, gluttony, sloth, pride, greed, envy, and wrath—have fascinated people with their exciting story lines. Shortly after we began working with legal teams to simplify their arguments, we realized that we could use these sins to help jurors recognize motivations.

It actually came to us as a result of the way the jurors themselves would interpret the facts of a case. We started to notice a pattern. The first time we'd meet with a legal team, they'd say something like, "This is a really complicated case, so try and follow." We would, and we'd present their arguments to our focus groups. At some point during the sessions, a participant would always say, "It's obvious the guy just wanted the money," or, "It all comes down to the guy was sleeping with his secretary." The jurors simplified the case into being about one of the base motivations, and they were usually right.

We decided to see if we could select sins that would fit various legal arguments before we presented the arguments to focus groups. A business-to-business case became a story about envy, not about whether decisions were made in the best interests of the company. A product liability case became a story about the pride of an engineer who refused to acknowledge that his design was dangerous. A legal malpractice case became the story of a slothful lawyer who failed to meet deadlines.

For pure telenovela-style drama with plenty of sin on both sides, it was hard to beat the case of the blackmailed doctor. "Dr. T" was an internist with a wife and a medical practice in a mid-size city on the East Coast. "Maureen" was an attractive thirty-something blonde whose videotaped deposition prompted one guy in our focus group to blurt out, "I'd want to be with that!" Maureen was suing Dr. T for malpractice, testifying that he had carried on an eighteen-month affair with her, prescribed massive amounts of medications (at least seventeen different painkillers and antidepressants), and generally exploited her fragile state of mind.

To help shape Dr. T's defense, we conducted focus groups with people from the town where the trial would be held. The mock jurors we interviewed all felt that it was unethical for Dr. T to have had a sexual relationship with a patient and to prescribe so many drugs. Then they learned that Maureen had been blackmailing the doctor for prescriptions, money, and ocean cruises, and that she had been planning to do so from her first visit to his office. We showed them some of the

Fatal Attraction–style emails Maureen had sent the doctor, such as: "DON'T forget the money and a refill for 150mg of Zoloft. Or my first call will be to your wife," and, "We *are* having coffee this morning. I don't care what you have to do. You will have coffee this morning or pay; that's not a threat, it's a *promise*."

Ultimately Maureen received drugs, money, and vacations totaling more than $300,000 from Dr. T before she filed her malpractice suit. As a result of his relationship with Maureen, Dr. T lost his job and his license to practice medicine in his home state. He had to move, take out a second mortgage on his home, and he almost lost his family.

The defense could not argue that Dr. T had acted appropriately by having a physical relationship with a patient, nor did it want to justify the number of prescriptions he wrote for Maureen. What the defense could do, however, was draw attention to Maureen's conduct. She had already received a substantial sum through her blackmail efforts, and it was also shown that she had refused therapy when it was offered to her. The jurors were left with a single logical motivation for her lawsuit: greed. The doctor's behavior was initially motivated by lust, another deadly sin jurors understood completely.

Once the jurors focused on these sins, they decided that Dr. T had already been punished enough for his transgressions. Maureen, however, had not been punished for hers. In our focus groups, the jurors took it upon themselves to punish her by siding with the defense. In real life, after learning how the defense planned to present their case, Maureen's attorneys agreed to settle out of court—a good result, considering the substantial awards that often go to plaintiffs in malpractice cases.

The moral of the story is that it was simple. Victory goes to the person who can tell a simple story that the audience will relate to. In business, the most popular story is "I will help you make [or save] money." There are other important stories about things like loyalty and satisfaction (customer, client, or employee), but if you want to get your audience's attention, it's the story about money that does the trick. As I mentioned in Power #1, even if making money seems like the obvious goal, it's still a good idea to say it out loud and make it the clear centerpiece of your business pitch.

POWER #12

Own the Language

In 1985, Starbucks was a lone coffee-bean shop in Seattle's Pike Place Market. It was manned by a few coffee-fanatic owners. No one outside of Italy knew what a *barista* was. Across America, beverages were sold in sizes small, medium, and large.

Today, Starbucks has more than fifteen thousand locations worldwide. When we conducted focus groups for a major condominium developer, people cited two conditions for any condo they might purchase: a parking space and a Starbucks within walking distance.

What had changed since 1985? Starbucks got all the way

inside our heads. They did it by selling tasty coffee in cozy stores, and by insisting that we use their complicated, small-is-tall *latte* lingo to order it. I've never worked for Starbucks, but as a marketing guy I know that when you own the language, you own the debate. Starbucks so thoroughly owns the language that we order a Venti even if we aren't in a Starbucks store. Right now, someone who needs caffeine is "making a Starbucks run." Starbucks doesn't just have a recognizable brand, it owns the *idea* of coffee.

It's a concept that has long been familiar to people in advertising. For them, the gold standard of owning the language has always been when the product name replaces the actual noun or verb. Classic examples are Kleenex for tissue, ChapStick for lip balm, FedEx for overnight delivery service, and Xerox for photocopy. These brands became the leaders in their markets because they controlled the terms. Recently, Apple has entered the master's circle by introducing the world to iPod, which begat podcasting. But for depth of influence, Starbucks is unmatched. Even when the company announced in 2008 that it was scaling back and shutting some stores, no one doubted the degree to which Starbucks has permanently infiltrated our language and altered our perception of coffee.

Politicians aim for the same buy-in when creating a piece of legislation. The average American opposes "welfare" and supports "a social safety net" (even though they are essentially the same thing), so bills and propositions are named accordingly. One of my earliest insights into the importance of controlling the terms came when I was twenty-four years old and working on my first political campaign. We were promoting the School Choice Initiative, which was essentially a voucher plan that would give parents $4,000 they could spend at any school. The teachers' unions, who opposed the initiative, had outspent us three- or four-to-one on TV and radio ads blasting the plan. As we were sitting around the table toward the end of the campaign, one of the staffers said, "I really think we can win this voucher initiative." It occurred to me that if our own staff was calling it "the voucher initiative," we were doomed. The other side had won the war of words, because people don't like vouchers and they do like school choice. "We're going to get slaughtered," I thought, and we did.

Your ability to invent the terms allows you to own the terms, and then everyone will adopt your way of thinking about the issue. In business, owning the language means that your product or service is the one people will remember. You don't necessarily need to hire a marketing team to do this—

every business has employees who create names for the work they do. To the extent that you can get your clients using those names, you'll be more successful.

John Ulitsch, marketing manager at Green Jobsites in Smyrna, Georgia, was fortunate enough to have an inspired employee give his new product a terrific name. Ulitsch had developed a truck-mounted grinding machine that converted waste lumber from construction projects into wood mulch. The mulch could then be used on site as lumber pads or for erosion control. There was strong demand for the huge grinder once builders realized that it was no more expensive than hauling the waste lumber to a landfill. With business booming, Ulitsch went to his employees and said, "We really have to come up with a name for this."

Operations manager Osberto Villanueva was quick on the uptake: "I was joking and I came out with this idea, 'Let's call it Godzilla . . . Godzilla . . . *Grindzilla!*'" The name instantly stuck. It's unforgettable and it perfectly describes the product.[1]

At Jury Impact, certain terms for our techniques have evolved and become selling points. When we're focus-grouping people, we use a scale of 1 to 5 to gauge which way the group is leaning on an issue. We christened this our Lean Scale. We sometimes give the participants a handheld dial that lets them rate the effectiveness of an argument. They dial a number that is fed into a computer in the room behind the mirror, where all the numbers are translated into a moving graph. Clients love it because it provides instant visual feedback on their legal arguments or ad campaigns. We dubbed those dials our Effectiveness Meters. It's like a name a kid would make up when playing mad scientist, but clients now ask us, "What are the Lean Scale questions? Are you bringing the Effectiveness Meters?" Naming things works. It makes them more important.

The Geek Squad

If your message plays to your audience's predispositions, you're halfway home. But what if those predispositions are negative? Shouldn't your goal be to disprove them somehow? Not necessarily. It's better to recognize your audience's reality and then turn the weakness into a strength. The right language can achieve that, and a prime example is the spectacular success of the Geek Squad. They truly own the language when it comes to fixing computers.

The Geek Squad was founded in 1994 by Robert Stephens, a twenty-three-year-old college student from Minneapolis who invested a mere $200 in his start-up. He knew the business had some weaknesses in the form of image problems: "One of the big complaints about people in our industry is that they have a big ego, they talk down to you, they're control freaks, maybe because people used to pick on them so much." Their reputation stank, and sometimes they did too. In fact, Stephens has consistently been quoted as saying that when he founded the Geek Squad, computer repairmen were generally seen as just a couple of steps up the food chain from plumbers. He needed a name for his company that would neutralize the negatives associated with the trade.[2]

That was challenge number one. Challenge number two was the fact that the fledgling organization consisted of a single employee, Stephens himself. He made house calls on his mountain bike. Stephens wanted a company name that would imply there was a whole crew of repairmen on call 24/7. Eventually lightning struck with "Geek Squad." "It was perfect," he told the *Minneapolis Star Tribune* in 1997. "It was action-oriented, eye-catching—and most important, it stuck in your memory."

The Geek Squad's name was the springboard for the company's brand, which is carried out visually in its cars (VW bugs painted police-cruiser black-and-white) and its signature uniform, a suit-and-tie combo inspired by a 1970 photo of NASA engineers at Mission Control. The Geeks, in their high-water pants, short-sleeved white shirts, and black nylon clip-on ties, look like NASA's brainy engineers combined with Cold War CIA agents. Squint your eyes and they look like the Blues Brothers. Stephens added a dash of detective by issuing his "agents" shiny ID badges right out of *Dragnet*. Andy Bork, the company's first official dispatcher, recalls that when hiring new employees, "The question always came up, 'Do I have to wear that?' Once they got it on and were amongst a dozen other people that had it on, it's all of a sudden a sign of coolness."[3]

Job titles at the Geek Squad extend the spy motif. Double Agents, Special Agents, and Secret Weapons are sent forth to repair computers. Covert Operators handle software problems over the phone. Public Defenders field customer service calls. At Geek Squad City in Louisville, Kentucky, where computers are repaired in a huge campuslike setting, the theme continues in a schizoid kind of way: part small town, part 1950s sci-fi movie, part Quantico. The city is run by a "mayor" and also boasts an "ambassador." Tables in the cafeteria are designated Earth, Pluto, and Saturn. One wall is labeled "City Council." Elsewhere, a closed door bears the warning "Super Secret Development Room. Unauthorized Entry Will Result in Pain or Death."

Dragnet lingo pervades every element of the organization, from its motto ("Serving the Public, Policing Technology and Protecting the World") to the narration on its official video ("Today we're everywhere, keeping the public under continuous surveillance and intervening when necessary") to the FAQs on its website ("The Geek Squad is comprised of highly trained and mobile individuals, or Agents, who are dedicated to making your computer(s) work properly. These people have banded together and sworn to rid the earth of inferior computer behavior.").[4]

Converting self-conscious computer geeks into smooth operators has always been one of Stephens' objectives, not only as a way to increase customer satisfaction—social skills matter—but also to improve his employees' quality of life. Turning the "weakness" of geekhood into the firm's biggest strength was a priority. In 2007 he jokingly told London's *Daily Telegraph*, "I look at geeks as a race of creatures and my goal is to kind of colonise them, and tap their power for the public good, promise to look after them, and take care of them, and not exploit them too much."[5] Indeed, the company's video proclaims that "Over the years we've also created a culture and mystique that has completely redefined the role of the geek in society." Stephens has always been aware not only of the customers' reality ("Computer guys are smelly geeks who are going to treat me like a moron") but also his employees' reality ("You may not want to date me, but you can't use your computer without me"). One of Stephens' early clients, Frank Bennet, recalls, "He called it the Geek Squad because he wanted people to be proud of the fact that they were geeks." The brilliance of the Geek Squad brand has a lot to do with Stephens' compassion for both the geeks and the customers.[6]

From the beginning, Stephens realized that the secret to making his company successful and his employees happy was a sense of humor. "I'm going to be dead in eighty years, so I want to have a little bit of fun," he told National Public Radio in 1997. The Geekmobiles are cute and the uniforms are hilarious, but the language is what holds the concept together. Within the organization, it reinforces the quirky essence of geekdom and makes it cool. Outside the company, the lingo has caught on with customers, who will typically refer to a Geek Squad repairman (or woman) as "my Geek." On every level, Geek Squad owns the language of its industry. Acquired by Best Buy in 2002, it now employs twelve thousand people around the world. Robert Stephens is still CEO and deeply committed to the company he founded with $200 and a mountain bike.

POWER #13

Use Emotional Language

You don't sell newspapers by writing about an accident. You sell newspapers by writing about a tragic accident. That's the power of emotional language. Emotional language creates a picture in people's minds, and that helps them connect with your idea on a deeper level than if they just agree with the facts. Politicians and marketers are old hands at using vivid language to tell their story, and journalists do it even when they're supposedly presenting an objective report. If a journalist wants to jolt the public into caring about a case of misdiagnosis, he or she will write something like, "A fist-size blood clot was developing." That factual yet gruesome description will grab readers' attention much more than "a five-inch blood clot." Good trial lawyers are skilled practitioners of emotional language too—ironic, since lawyers are also the folks who brought you legalese.

Using emotional language is a way to get your audience not only to understand your argument but also to feel it. A few years ago I was involved in a campaign for a bill to fund an extra lane for a local freeway, and the county wanted to run promotional ads for the bill promising to "improve our roads" and "reduce commute time." Folks might like the idea of that, but they won't necessarily bother to leave the house to go vote for it. People don't care about traffic unless they are stuck in it and missing their children's soccer practice. A better approach was to run ads asking, "Wouldn't it be nice to get to your child's practice on time for once?" or, "Wouldn't you like to get home early enough to have dinner with your family every night?" That helped voters picture exactly how the expanded freeway would improve their lives.

Emotional language is specific. If I told you, "Cloverdale Enterprises gave $10,000 to the community," you'd probably think, "That's nice," and if you pictured anything it would be $10,000 disappearing into the black hole of city government. But if I said, "Cloverdale Enterprises handed out bottled water at the city's 10K, repaved the high school's tennis courts, and sponsored a holiday food drive at the elementary school," you'd instantly visualize the Cloverdale folks handing water bottles to thirsty runners, followed by images of tennis-playing high schoolers and cute third graders loading up food boxes. Those things together may not cost $10,000, but they paint a picture. It's personal, it's specific, and it's meaningful. Whenever you want to use emotional language, you need to ask yourself, "What is the most basic and specific way this issue can affect the average person's everyday life?"

Using emotional language sometimes sparks the accusation that facts are being "spun." But in every situation, each side has its version of the truth. Attorneys have an obligation to talk about the truth in a way that benefits their client. Likewise, anyone who hopes to persuade an audience has an obligation to explain his or her version of the situation in language the audience will understand, remember, and care about.

Consider a case we worked on that involved a premature infant who had developed learning disabilities. He was one of a set of triplets, and the parents were suing the hospital where the mom had given birth, claiming that this infant had been treated differently from his siblings in the neonatal unit. As consultants to the defense team, our job was to help jurors understand that an infant as fragile as this one might have difficulty surviving at all, let alone without some type of disability. In describing the baby, we could have said, "The child measured 15.25 centimeters and weighed 110 grams at birth," which was what the physician had recorded. Instead we said, "This infant was the size of a stick of butter." That was a shocking and vivid picture, and it was also true. It instantly told jurors exactly how small the baby was. They could see it. They would remember it. They could reason for themselves that such a child would be at risk in the best of circumstances. And jurors didn't have to do calculations in their heads to figure it out, which meant they could easily follow our attorneys' argument as it continued.

Sometimes you'll find yourself arguing *against* powerful emotional language. We once were hired to defend a hospital whose ER had briefly treated a homeless man, then released him onto the street, where he promptly died of pneumonia on the hospital's front steps. A terrible situation was made worse by the ER doctor's flippant comment, which she actually wrote on the patient's chart: "Diagnosis: Acute homelessness." Those callous words could have cost the hospital millions, if it weren't for the fact that the people suing the hospital—the man's estranged children—were even more callous than the doctor, and the jury didn't want to "reward" them. But the potentially damning power of those two words wasn't lost on any of us.

One bit of emotional language I got a kick out of occurred right after Barack Obama was elected president. In the earliest days of his presidency, he fielded a lot of questions about which is better, big government or small government. Obama said, "I think what the American people want more than anything is just common sense, smart government." Who could argue with that—or define it? But it feels so right. Obama was doing what savvy communicators do all the time: describing an object or idea as if it were human. Intelligence is a human attribute, and by saying, "Government can be smart," he just brought it to life. A living thing is emotional; a bureaucracy is not.

Sommeliers are masters of this art. When they're telling you about wine, they'll say, "It's refined. It's demure." If they said, "This wine is delicious," it would mean nothing. If they say, "This wine starts out shy, but it really opens up," those are human descriptions that spark an emotional response.

You can use the technique anywhere. If you're reviewing a document, instead of telling the author, "Nice job," you can say, "This is an intelligent piece of work." If a staffer has arranged a luncheon for your clients, you can say, "That's a very elegant buffet." You might not tell the person, "You're so elegant," but you can say it about the buffet, and they'll get the same good feeling. That's using emotional language.

A Reporter's Notes on Emotional Language

When I hired Claire Luna to work for Jury Impact, it was in part because of her experience as a journalist for the *Los Angeles Times*. Her beat covered the criminal court system, which gave her valuable insights about jurors. During her years at the *Times*, Claire was witness to many natural disasters as well as disturbing criminal trials. I wondered about how she covered those stories and how her editors felt about emotional language.

Claire told me that editors encourage reporters to use emotional language as long as the words are as accurate as possible. All writers are taught to show and not tell—you don't say, "The mother was sad," you use verbs and details that provide that information without being obvious about it. Was the distraught mother "holding" her son's photograph, or was she "clutching" it? Verbs are every professional writer's most powerful weapon when it comes to packing an emotional punch.

Providing specific details creates a picture for readers and makes them feel as if they're part of the story. That involves using all the senses, not just the visual. Claire recalled, "Once I wrote about a monastery in San Diego, and I described it as being within a jet's roar of Camp Pendleton. That kind of detail is accurate, and it also paints a picture of the silent monks padding around the monastery as the jets roar in the distance. You instantly feel the clash between the two worlds."

I asked Claire how journalists interview emotional people—folks who are grieving, stressed, or somehow traumatized. There are times both at work and in your personal life when you need to ask people delicate questions, and I wondered if any of the reporter's methods could translate to those situations.

Claire told me that when approaching someone who is under stress, for instance a person involved in a trial, there's a warming-up process you have to go through first because people are afraid of being judged. To get to the desired comfort level, she would talk to them in the same way they were talking to her. "I'd try to get a sense of what their lives were like, so when they said, 'Man, this trial is going on forever,' I could say, 'Yeah. That must be hard, especially with your little girl just starting kindergarten and your older one in softball.' Then they would understand that I cared about the details, and that I knew there was other stuff going in their lives that shaped what they brought to the table."

When Claire was working on a fresh story and had no background on the people, she used a different approach. One rule always applied: She didn't settle for the first answer she got. "You have to keep asking questions, no matter how difficult or delicate it is. When I was interviewing a stranger and I didn't have time to warm them up, I would ask for specifics. I've found that, especially when you're dealing with delicate topics, it's easier for people to deal in specifics than in big blanket statements like 'How do you feel?' When you ask those bigger questions, you're typically going to get simple answers like 'I'm sad.' So in a situation where you're interviewing someone who just lost their home to a fire, you would ask, 'What did you lose that you're going to miss most? What part of your house would you have gone to for comfort had it still been standing?' Specific questions like that get specific, detailed answers, and that is where you'll find the emotion."

One of the most important things Claire learned as a reporter was to be concise. One or two really good quotes are a lot more poignant and effective than five or six quotes that restate the same information. This is true of presentations too, especially in PowerPoint. "Sometimes people put up a PowerPoint slide and it's chock-full of text, and the meaning of what they're trying to convey is completely lost," said Claire. "Another interesting thing I've noticed about PowerPoints is that people rarely use quotes in the slides, and quotes are a great way to get third-party credibility up in front of an audience. Just remember to edit them so they aren't too long. As a reporter you learn to edit yourself, and that's incredibly valuable in communication. Less is usually better."

POWER #14

Make Sure Everyone's Invested

Want people to be more enthusiastic about your plan? Make it their idea. The way to make this happen is to create situations that will encourage the others to speak up, pro or con. I've found five tactics that are especially effective in getting people to participate and become invested.

The first tactic is simply to ask questions, staying alert to answers that align with what you hope to accomplish. In most situations there are not infinite possibilities, so if you ask the right questions, sooner or later someone is going to respond with the answers that support your goal, at which point you can agree with him or her. Now it's that person's idea too.

Let's say you're the editor of your organization's weekly e-bulletin. People from various departments send you material, but lately the bulletin has become a depository for too many nonessential articles. You feel that it's getting too long and recipients are going to start trashing it before they even open it. So you call a meeting of department heads, with the goal of setting limits on the topics you will accept. Instead of simply announcing that goal, you could approach it in a more open-ended way by saying, "I've called this meeting to get your input on how we can improve the bulletin." Then you can ask for suggestions. You listen carefully; they might have some excellent ideas you hadn't thought of. When someone says something that applies to the specific problem you're trying to solve—for example, if Martin says, "The bulletin just seems so confusing"—you can agree and encourage him to elaborate: "I know what you mean. Do you think we should limit the topics? If so, what topics would you like to see?"

Another approach is to give them specific choices. As we mentioned in Powers #7 and #10, people like having options. In the meeting about the bulletin, if your goal is to set limits on the types of articles you will accept, you could ask the group to prioritize three types: "Which of the following three topics is most important: upcoming events, new products, or media coverage?" The truth may be that any order would be fine with you—three specific topics would be a huge improvement over the scattershot material you currently receive. By getting them to concentrate on choices you preselected, you have already achieved your goal of limiting the topics.

Another technique is to use their small point to support your big goal. This is a matter of being alert to everything the others are saying. Maybe during the discussion of how confusing the current bulletin is, Gina observes, "The font is too small." Technically that's a graphic design issue and doesn't have anything to do with content. But you can use it to support your goal: "You could be right about that. A larger font would be easier for some people to read, and that would definitely improve the bulletin." Your mission is to make everyone in the room feel that their input is valued, because it is. You can decide later whether or not to change the font size, but it's a worthy suggestion.

Another effective tactic is to tie your points together using other people's suggestions. Let's take the above example a step further to illustrate. When Gina says, "The font is too small," instead of commenting on it yourself, refer to other people's comments: "That goes back to what Martin said about our need to clarify the bulletin because it's too confusing. A larger font could definitely improve the clarity. And when we relate that to Bill's suggestions about making the headlines shorter, we're really homing in on the clarity issue." Now you've gotten Gina, Martin, and Bill invested in the changes.

Another way to make your listeners feel invested in the goal is to use their language to describe it. It can be subtle, like using the term *font* instead of *typeface* because Gina called it a font. Or you can repeat their statements back to them: "So what I'm hearing you say, Bill, is that long headlines are annoying and you like to read short, sweet headlines. Right?" You can also adopt a term they came up with as part of the unofficial lingo of the project, even if it's kind of playful: "From now on, all headlines will be short and sweet." It makes people feel good; it boosts their egos.

The ultimate in using your listeners' language is adopting a phrase they come up with as an important official element of the project. In the case of the bulletin, it could be a tagline that runs right under the bulletin's name, or it could even be the name itself. Naming things is powerful, as I mentioned in "Own the Language." The person who provides a new name for the bulletin will feel especially connected to it.

So if someone comes up with a brilliant new name, consider changing it even if you're the editor and it wasn't your idea. That's a beautiful example of setting aside your ego, and it will win you big points in the eyes of your colleagues.

Matching the Voters' Ideas with Obama's Message

During the presidential campaign of 2008, I had an inside view of how the teams behind John McCain and Barack Obama were developing their messages. More than any slogan since Ronald Reagan's "It's Morning in America," Barack Obama's "Hope and Change" connected with voters. You can bet the Obama team was listening very closely to what people wanted to hear and repeating it back to them, tweaking it week by week.

The Obama folks were dedicated and zealous focus-groupers. I know because I was conducting focus groups on behalf of the Republicans and John McCain. Every city has focus group rental facilities that contain all the necessary equipment—conference rooms with one-way mirrors, microphone and camera setups, and so forth. It's specialized equipment, so everyone who conducts focus groups usually ends up using the same facilities. Inevitably, when I would arrive in a city and start setting up in one of the facilities, the people staffing it would say, "The Obama people were just here."

Change was the buzzword throughout the campaign, introduced by Obama at the beginning. In the first few weeks of the McCain campaign I would ask my focus groups, "What does *change* mean?" And they couldn't define it. I could see that the Obama team was going to have to back off *change* because voters didn't know what it meant. Then I would hear Barack in his speeches and commercials say, "Change means nothing without specifics. That's why you need to see my plan." He was repeating back what he'd heard from his focus groups.

Early on in the campaign, the focus groups were telling us, "We can't have another George Bush," which was what Barack Obama was saying in his speeches. McCain began to separate himself from George Bush, telling voters, "I took on Bush about climate control, about immigration, about campaign finance," emphasizing big issues that divided him from the Republican Party. When I reminded the focus groups about this, they'd say, "Yeah, but his economic policies are the same." Practically the next day, I'd hear Obama on the stump saying, "We can't have four more years of the failed economic policies of George Bush." Obama stopped saying that McCain was just like George Bush, and switched to saying that his economic policies were like Bush's. It was a tactical decision based on what he'd heard in polling and focus groups, and it helped carry him to victory in 2008.

POWER #15

Get Third-Party Validation

Few people want to be the first to agree with someone else's idea. At the same time, nobody wants to be the last on board. Most people like to be in the middle yet toward the front. Providing third-party validation can help people overcome their fear of being first. There are lots of ways to subtly inject the third party into your conversation:

"One of the reasons John and I hooked up . . ."

"I think the production department liked this idea so much because . . ."

"One of the things the *L.A. Times* said about our project was . . ."

"The reason we've got so many good quotes on that website is . . ."

You don't want to be too heavy-handed about it, because then it could be taken as a challenge—"John agrees with me, so why don't you?" What you're doing is casually letting your audience know that someone else has already looked at your plan and thinks it's good.

In politics, third-party validation is called "earned media," meaning you don't have to pay for it like you do for advertising. It can be an editorial, a newspaper's endorsement, a feature story, or the results of a poll that's been conducted by a nonpartisan organization such as Gallup or Zogby. Politicians also call on individuals to provide third-party credibility—union heads, community leaders, local celebrities, other politicians. Private groups can play a crucial third-party role as well; think Swift Boat Veterans attacking John Kerry. In court, the third-party validators are expert witnesses. In product advertising, it's "three out of four dentists," or a celebrity or sports star. Ever notice how many awards there are for automotive excellence? They provide third-party credibility for auto manufacturers.

One of my first jobs in politics was as an intern for a U.S. senator. This was before cable networks had expanded, and the Big Three network news stations were the only real game in town. My senator couldn't get any coverage in the L.A.

media market. It was during the first Gulf War, and he was going to be marching in a parade on behalf of the troops. I called the local CBS affiliate and said, "Do you want to interview him?"

"No, we don't have time," they told me.

I called ABC and they said the same thing. When I called NBC, I changed tactics.

"Hey, I've got CBS and ABC slotted for one o'clock and one-thirty. Do you want twelve-thirty?"

"We'll take it," they said.

I called CBS back and said, "ABC just confirmed for twelve-thirty. Do you want one o'clock?"

"We do," they said.

Finally, I called ABC again and told them, "CBS and NBC have him; do you want him?"

"Absolutely."

No one wants to be first or last, but everybody likes running in the pack.

In business, your third-party validators may be colleagues who want to share the credit for your idea. In practical terms, this could be a smart move, because successful persuasion is all about building a coalition. It will be a good trade-off if you get results more quickly.

For example, when I present the results of my focus groups,

I could take all the credit by reporting on what *I* have deduced from *my* focus group that *I* designed and conducted. But that isn't the most effective way, and it risks setting up a me-against-my-clients situation if the focus group data is not what the clients want to hear. Instead, to sidestep the clients' egos and build third-party credibility, I'll remind them, "It's not my opinion; it's the room's opinion. Eleven out of twelve people agreed that the case seems frivolous, and that's probably what you're going to face in court." It's even more persuasive when I name individual participants: "I think the most interesting point was raised by Kim, who said that the doctor looks 'kindly.' It built on Marco's theory that everyone hates their health insurance company but loves their doctor. Which goes to our overall concern: The jury probably will not believe this particular pediatrician was capable of gross negligence." The focus group is third-party credibility, and I've used the participants' words to make my point.

Third-party validation is a huge advantage at fund-raising events. Whether you're raising money for a new playground at your child's school or for the next presidential candidate, you'll find the same "not me first" attitude in any group of potential donors. The time-tested way of dealing with this is to find someone before the meeting who will promise to make the first donation. Then you know that at some point this person is going to stand up and say, "I love what you're planning. Count me in for five hundred dollars," or, "I'm in for a hundred and I'll match five other people here for another hundred." This is not somebody whose arm you've twisted; it's someone who was going to support your cause anyway. You're just making sure they speak up at the most beneficial time.

If you don't have anybody lined up to support you, the best way to get third-party validation is by using the Internet. Search for whatever it is you're proposing, and within minutes you'll have something you can work with. A half hour on Google is all it takes for my team to come up with third-party validation for almost any issue we're promoting. With a little more time, you can search for your topic in op-ed pieces, trade journal reports, think tanks, government agencies, studies, and surveys. There is almost always an expert or an official study from which you can get a compelling fact or number (I'll talk about how to use statistics and other numbers in the next chapter).

J.D. Power and the Ultimate Third Party

For third-party credibility, it's hard to beat thousands of satisfied customers. Since the 1970s, J.D. Power and Associates has been conducting customer-satisfaction surveys, and since 1984 they've been presenting awards across a wide range of industries, most notably automobiles. The company calls itself "the voice of the consumer," and its award and logo are prized advertising tools. The success of J.D. Power provides an interesting glimpse into the enormous value businesses place on third-party credibility.

James David ("Dave") Power started his company in 1968 at his kitchen table, with his wife helping him tabulate survey responses. At the time, market research involved working for only one client within an industry, and it usually meant providing that client with information that would support whatever they were already doing. Power's brainstorm was to design and conduct an auto industry customer-satisfaction survey independently, without being tied to any one automaker client. He then published the results and sold them to whoever was interested. His survey did not involve experts or tests—just responses from people who owned and drove the vehicles he was studying.

Power's business took off in 1971, when he received a call from the Detroit office of the *Wall Street Journal*, which had got hold of a copy of a J.D. Power report that exposed problems in a particular engine. They wanted him to confirm the report, which he did. "The next day, on the front page of the

Wall Street Journal was the article. Within 48 hours, we were in every newspaper in the world," Power recalled in a 2001 interview.[1] That article solidified J.D. Power as an automotive industry influencer, and in the decades since, the company has expanded its surveys to include electronics, health care, finance, insurance, and more. J.D. Power awards have become highly coveted by the industries they cover.

How valuable is that third-party stamp of approval? One former J.D. Power employee, who asked that I not use his name, recalled the lengths to which some automakers would go in order to secure a high ranking: "A lot of companies will hire statisticians to dig in and find out how they weight the answers. They'll try to game the system. I knew of companies that would say, 'Hey, the J.D. Power survey is going out next week, so let's send cookies to all the customers who bought cars during the months that they're going to be surveying.' It's created a whole sub-industry to game the survey. If you put that much effort into actually creating customer satisfaction, you wouldn't have to worry."

This insider also wondered how many consumers were aware that the surveys only measure customer satisfaction. "A lot of people are confused. They think Dave Power is walking around in his little white coat with a clipboard and personally reviewing these products. It's a survey, and as a survey it's open to the standard errors that you get in surveys. One thing that really makes industry people mad is that J.D. Power names only one winner. This is *the* top company in quality. But in reality the difference between *the* top company and maybe the top six or eight companies is not statistically valid. . . . The company line is, 'Well, in a horse race if three horses are really close, only one wins.' So companies fight for those rankings. They mean a lot to them." So much, in fact, that the winners of the J.D. Power awards are willing to pay licensing fees to J.D. Power for the right to display those awards in their advertising. That's right: Companies cannot display an image of the J.D. Power award they won unless they pay J.D. Power a fee. And they do it, all for the ultimate in third-party credibility.

POWER #16

Get a Couple of Numbers

One of my favorite ways to open a speech is by announcing, "Eighty-two percent of the public will believe any made-up statistic." Forty-five minutes later I'll come back and ask the audience, "What percentage of people will remember any made-up statistic?" And the whole crowd will shout, "Eighty-two!" Everyone remembers one or two numbers, but no one remembers many more than that. It's worth a few minutes of research to get a couple of numbers before you make your pitch.

Advertisers have long recognized the near-magical selling power of numbers, especially weird ones. In 1879, Ivory Soap was boasting about being "99 and 44/100% pure," whatever that means, and the current ad campaign for Miller Genuine Draft beer is based on its having 64 calories. By the time you read this there will be another batch of number-based campaigns. Even this book is called *27 Powers of Persuasion*. Part of the reason for getting a couple of numbers is to add another type of third-party credibility to your pitch; part of the reason is to have some hard data with which to arm your advocates, as we'll read about in the next chapter; and part is simply because numbers are easy to remember, helping to burn your idea into the minds of your listeners.

You'll usually see numbers presented in one of the following ways: as a single impressive amount (over 10 million sold!), as a comparison (3 out of 4 dentists prefer Colgate), or as a percentage (the president has a 63 percent approval rating). As a businessperson, the best way to present numbers often depends on what's available to you. If you have the resources to run a survey with one thousand people, and eight hundred of them love your product, you're in luck—that's an overwhelming number. If you go down to the street in front of your building and interview ten strangers and eight of them love the product, it's technically the same ratio but obviously not as impressive. So you could say, "Eighty percent of the people I interviewed loved it," or "Eight out of ten people thought it was great." If the specific number strikes you as significant, use it. If not, convert it to a comparison or a percentage.

Where do you get numbers, aside from conducting your own informal poll? First think about any positive numbers associated with your business. You only need one or two of them. Do you have a 90 percent return rate with your clients? Did you receive ten letters from satisfied customers within a single month? Has your business been featured in five local news stories over the past year? Think about successes in any aspect of your business, and then determine if there are any numbers associated with those successes.

Another way to find useful numbers is to broaden your search beyond your own business to the field in general. For instance, if you offer math tutoring, you can find statistics about its general effect on students' grades or test scores. (Such as, "Students who get tutored generally perform 20 percent higher on their SATs.") Go online and you'll find all sorts of research studies, customer satisfaction surveys, and so forth that will provide the numbers you need. The University of Michigan Institute for Social Research is home to a mammoth collection of social research surveys, which it has been conducting for more than fifty years. Its website, www.isr.umich.edu, will take you to valuable data on consumer attitudes, income, and much more. For straight-up demographic statistics, the U.S. Census Bureau (www.census.gov) is a gold mine.

Understandably, audiences and consumers are sometimes skeptical of numbers. The media regularly misuses them to scare viewers into paying attention. Every year, when there is a slow news cycle or a particularly alarming child kidnapping case, parents are treated to scare stories about child abduction that are inevitably "supported" by misleading numbers. In September 2009, as children were returning to school, NBC's *Today Show* played into parents' fears by citing the National Center for Missing & Exploited Children's statistic that "39% of all abductions occur walking to and from school." After the piece and during the discussion with his guests, Al Roker, to his credit, stated that "a lot of these fears are irrational, because of the 60 million kids in the U.S. under the age of fifteen, only 115 children were taken, and when we hear a statistic that almost 40 percent of kids have been abducted, that's an alarming, maybe misleading statement." So we're talking 39 percent of 115 children, which is about 45 children out of 60 million. Meaning there is less than a one in a million chance your child will be abducted while walking to school.

No wonder people are sometimes wary of numbers. But despite the potential for abuse, numbers remain powerful tools for persuading an audience. The key is to use them responsibly, and in order to do that, you need a bit of background on what survey statistics do and do not mean.

The studies you'll find when you are researching statistics will either be *quantitative* or *qualitative*. Quantitative studies ask straightforward questions like "Who will you vote for?" They rely purely on the number (quantity) of respondents, and in those studies, the minimum sample size needed for a statistically reliable result is three hundred. If you interview only one hundred people, you can be plus or minus 12 percent, and that means there's a 24 percent window of error, which is too large to be credible.

Qualitative surveys involve more in-depth interviewing. Their value comes from the amount and quality of information rather than the number of respondents. Even if relatively few people are surveyed, the statistics are still very useful. It definitely adds credibility to be able to say, "In all five focus groups, at least 9 out of 12 people preferred our product." Qualitative surveys have the added benefit of providing quotes from the participants that can be used as third-party validation.

When you do collect some numbers, keep in mind that in order to be effective they must be numbers average people can instantly comprehend, which means not too big and in a unit (dollars, miles, pounds) familiar to them. For instance, while politicians need to talk about the huge federal deficit, "billions" and "trillions" are incomprehensible sums. They are impossible to visualize, even with tricks like "If you lined all those dollars up they could reach to the moon and back!" The only way humans can grasp numbers is in human terms, which is why politicians will sometimes refer to the deficit in terms of how much each family would theoretically owe if we were all forced to pay down the debt equally. "Every family in America would have to pay $8,000" is a number you can envision. It's a number that you've managed. And you know how hard it is to earn and save that amount.

Winning Numbers

Tony Russo is president of Apex, a Sacramento PR firm specializing in public/political affairs, and the former president of Voter Connect Communications Inc., where he directed strategic planning and budgeting for corporate clients and political candidate campaigns. I asked him how he had used numbers in some of those campaigns. He told me, "One thing we started doing probably fifteen years ago is adding detail to our messages, so that people could believe them, understand them, and relate to them. Rather than just say, 'We're going to make schools better,' we would add statistics and say, 'California schools are in the bottom 10 percent nationally in test scores, and that's why we need education reform.'"

Almost any issue can be enhanced by the appropriate statistics. While creating a campaign for Hawaii's first woman governor, Republican Linda Lingle, Russo developed ads that repeatedly mentioned that Democrats had held the reins of power there for forty years. The campaign used statistics to talk about Hawaii's bad economy, jobless rate, student test scores, and school overcrowding. Ads showed pictures of school facilities that were in need of repair, and the point was driven home by numbers—the percentage or the actual number of classrooms that were in bad shape.

"Numbers provide evidence that our argument is, in fact, correct," notes Russo. "Most people aren't going to go do the counter-research to determine if it's correct or not." That said, he warns never to fudge the numbers. "Nothing undermines your argument more than using a bad number. If somebody disproves just one of your numbers, all of a sudden you've lost all your credibility."

Russo has observed that in political campaigns some of the most effective numbers are trends, such as the percentage that crime has gone up or down since the last election, and comparisons to other states. Being number one in homicides (California) or number fifty in high school graduates (Texas) is a shocking number for citizens to confront. In Mississippi, the heaviest state in the union, one out of every four people is obese. Those numbers paint a picture that makes the issue more personal to voters.[1]

As for recent campaign trends, Russo says, "A number I've seen lately that sticks with people is the percentage of dollars that are 'wasted'—or that's how it's portrayed—on administration and overhead. People think overhead is wasteful, and any numbers tied to waste and inefficiency are hitting home in the current economy."

POWER #17

Arm Your Advocates

In political campaigns, surrogate speakers are given daily talking points—succinct messages that help support the larger story. In the courtroom, attorneys repeat brief, memorable versions of their most effective arguments so that jurors can easily recall them later, when they're deliberating among themselves. The same strategy works in business settings. In most of those situations, you will have people who agree with you, people who don't, and the "undecideds" who will often tip the scale one way or another. Arming your advocates means making sure that those who agree with you have the information they need to influence other people, either when you're not around or when you're in a meeting and need a show of support. You can give different advocates different talking points, but don't give any one person more than three. Talking points can be about:

- Statistics, trends, or other numbers: "The number of people buying this type of software goes up ten percent each year."
- Third-party validation: "The legal department said this deal is bulletproof."
- Track record: "This division met or beat every deadline over the past six months."
- Experience: "Marissa has more knowledge about this field than anyone else in the company."

Any strong endorsement of your position can be a talking point, as long as it's brief and specific. Brevity is important not only so your advocates can remember your talking points but also so that the folks *they're* talking to can remember them (as you'll see in the story about Mazda on page 123).

Talking points work wonders in nonbusiness situations too. Say you're trying to convince your extended family to vacation in Austin. You might ask yourself, "What do most of the people in my family enjoy in a vacation?" Maybe it's good Mexican food and hiking. So you do a little research and get your talking points: "There are seven Mexican restaurants within a few blocks of downtown Austin. And a huge state park within city limits, including hiking trails with two waterfalls." You give these talking points to the people who like the idea of Austin and urge them to tell the family members who are on the fence. They can get it across in an abbreviated version: "Seven Mexican restaurants. A state park with two waterfalls!" It's just like a political campaign—you're using talking points to fuel the base and convince the undecideds.

Talking points are amazingly potent. Perhaps the most notorious example is the line Johnnie Cochran kept repeating during the 1995 trial of O. J. Simpson: "If it doesn't fit, you must acquit." Simpson was on trial for murdering his wife, Nicole, and her friend Ron Goldman, but Cochran built his defense of O.J. around the Los Angeles Police Department's reputation for treating African Americans unfairly. One piece of evidence was a bloody glove that Detective Mark Fuhrman said he had discovered on the Simpson estate. Fuhrman had been accused of making racist statements in the past, and according to Cochran, that proved the detective was an untrustworthy witness. When Simpson attempted to put the glove on his hand at the trial and claimed it was too small, Cochran alleged that Fuhrman had planted it on the estate. Fuhrman's testimony was central to the prosecution, claimed Cochran, and "If it doesn't fit, you must acquit."[1]

O. J. Simpson was found not guilty. The day after the trial, juror Brenda Moran gave a press conference explaining why she had voted to set Simpson free. Her closing words were, "The simple thing, I'm gonna leave this with you and then, I'm outta here. In plain English, the glove didn't fit."[2]

Getting Mazda Out of a Rut

One of the most common persuasion challenges in large organizations involves trying to convince the old guard that they need a new marketing approach. This thankless task often falls to outside advertising agencies. Those who know how to arm advocates within the organization have the best chance of moving the powers that be.

In the late 1990s, Eric Landau* found himself in that situation while he was working at the ad agency Foote, Cone & Belding (FC&B). Mazda was a longtime client, and Landau was on the account. The automaker had used a very conservative, traditional advertising message for many years—their typical television spot had a family man describing a sedan as "smooth, quiet, solid, and roomy," or observing its "great road manners, plus impressive mileage." Mazda's most animated jingle bragged, "Sakes alive! Only Mazda's got a sporty truck for just $5,795." The brand positioning was that with Mazda you got a fully loaded vehicle for the same price as other brands' stripped-down vehicles.

"It was an effective sales message, but it didn't create any imagery," Landau recalls. "It wasn't doing anything to elevate the brand." More problematic was that, as the nineties progressed, the message was less and less true. Mazdas were becoming ever more expensive. "That message just wasn't going to hold up forever," says Landau. "We had to shift to a more emotional appeal."

FC&B presented their ad campaigns to the top American executives at Mazda, who in turn had to get them approved

* Not his real name.

by the company's Japanese owners. In 1999 they created an entirely different, more emotional campaign. It was based on research they did with "Mazda Maniacs"—people who had owned two, three, sometimes four Mazdas in a row, and who raved about the thrilling experience the vehicle delivered. "We wanted our campaign to capture that childlike feeling of sports car exhilaration," recalls Landau. "We knew it would be a radical departure. The company was being run by old-school car guys who said, 'You've got to show customers what they'll get for their money. There needs to be a list of features you can put in the newspapers.'"

Landau's team prepared for the inevitable resistance by creating two separate campaigns. One continued the traditional, value-oriented theme. The other would eventually be launched with a commercial that asked, "What would happen if an SUV were raised by a family of sports cars?" In that ad, a Mazda SUV whips around a twisty country road, weaving in and out of a fleet of speeding sports cars. The lighting is intense, the landscape surreal, and storm clouds are roiling overhead. As the SUV tears past a young schoolboy, the boy turns to the camera and whispers, *"Zoom, zoom."* It was a highly emotional concept, tapping into every young male's infatuation with fast cars.

How did Landau's team convince the old guard to accept such a radical idea? First they gathered a lot of data from those surveys of "Mazda Maniacs." Then they created an ad from existing Mazda footage that approximated the ad they were pitching, showed it to focus groups of consumers, and collected their positive reactions. "We took edits from the focus groups of people saying things like, 'Wow, this makes me think so differently about Mazda,' and Mazda owners saying things like, 'This really captures the essence of how I feel about my vehicle.' So we had third-party endorsement of the idea." Armed with all that positive feedback, they approached people within Mazda whom they knew had been itching for a change in branding.

"They were all over it," says Landau. "This is exactly what they had been wanting for a long time, but never could convince anyone to do. So on one hand there was the grassroots approach of getting people to support the idea, and on the other hand there was a pretty serious consumer research effort."

Before the big presentation, Landau armed the advocates within Mazda. "We told them, 'It would be really helpful if you supported us. Here are some of the things you can say: It's a more emotionally driven message, which can lead to people buying with their heart instead of their pocketbooks, which will help overcome resistance to higher prices. It's more consistent with a future direction of the products. It's going to be more differentiating for the brand. It's a message that's hard to copy.'"

At the meeting, Landau and his team presented both campaigns. They offered only highlights of their focus group research, holding back the details so they would have something more to present if the execs wanted a second meeting. Then they sat back and let the advocates speak up.

"It was, I think, very effective to have the advocates start the positive discussion," says Landau. "They built on each other, and then all of a sudden you could see that they all started to convince themselves that this was a good idea. It became more *their* idea. They talked themselves into it versus us selling it to them."

The executives didn't buy the campaign at that first meeting, but they didn't kill it either. "That was a major victory," Landau recalls. "The one guy who wasn't ready to buy off on it right that minute said, 'You've given us a lot to think about. We want to be able to regroup and have a little more internal discussion.' Then we offered, 'Could we come back and show you some of the research results?' We had a second meeting and showed some of the videotape of the respondents. Again, they didn't decide right at that meeting. The important thing was having these advocates who were in meetings that we weren't in, who we were hoping could keep the fire alive in some of the internal discussions. And that seems to be exactly what happened."

Mazda's first "Zoom, zoom" commercial, featuring a catchy Brazilian song, aired in 2000. The "Zoom, zoom" theme was still going strong ten years later, making it one of the most enduring campaigns in the history of automotive marketing.

POWER #18

Aim for the Undecideds

Whether you need to convince twelve colleagues, twelve jurors, or 12 million voters, the most important people are usually the undecideds. In any group, there will be some who side with you from the beginning (unless your idea is very risky or radical), and there will be at least a few who are against you, if for no other reason than that they are naturally skeptical. Getting a few undecideds to shift in your direction is often all it takes to win the day.

If you doubt the importance of undecideds, think about all those extreme political messages from both the left and the right. They're intended to keep the base fueled, but the real target audience is the undecideds. The American Tort Reform Association (ATRA) will go looking for the silliest lawsuits in America and send them to radio stations across the land, where the shocking details will be broadcast to people who might not have cared much about frivolous lawsuits until they hear about that one outrageous example (remember McDonalds' hot coffee?). That's why groups from ATRA to PETA keep publicizing extreme examples of their cause. They're trying to influence the undecideds and get them to care.

That's a challenge when persuading undecideds—often they just don't care very much. They register as independents. Sometimes they vote, but often they don't bother. They don't pay as much attention as their more opinionated brethren. If forced to make a decision, as they are in focus groups or on juries, they tend to see things negatively or to see both sides to a fault.

Who are the undecideds? To get a clearer sense of them, we ran some numbers on juror malleability. A few patterns emerged:

- Jurors over fifty were about 10 percent more likely not to change their vote.

- Jurors without high school diplomas were about 15 percent more malleable.
- Women were 5 percent more malleable than men (this is very close to the margin of error).
- African Americans were 12 percent more malleable than whites and Latinos.
- Self-described "Moderate" and "Very Conservative" jurors were the most malleable, and "Very Liberal" jurors the least.
- Independents were about 10 percent more malleable than either Republican or Democratic jurors.

We don't know if these findings are true for groups outside the jury room, but some of the data mirrors the accepted wisdom in advertising. For instance, older people are assumed to be less willing to try new products than those under thirty. It's food for thought when you're trying to figure out who will be open to changing their minds. Beyond these patterns, we haven't been able to "profile" undecideds, but we do understand the strategy that is most effective in winning them over.

First, recognize that there will always be the three coalitions: for you, against you, and undecided. Forget about trying to make your opposition fall in love with you. Lee Atwater once said that George H. W. Bush could walk on water and the next day the media would report, "Bush Can't Swim," and he was right. Your ego may whisper, "If you're good enough, you'll be able to make *everyone* agree with you." But that's impossible. They never will. So you need to get over that and prepare for the undecideds.

Winning the undecideds requires subtlety. You can't just go around the room asking direct questions of the individuals who haven't voiced an opinion, and then prod them until they take a stand. Instead, you must earn their trust by talking to the other people in the group and letting the undecideds witness the action from the sidelines. The secret lies in how you handle your opposition. The best method is to incorporate their view, then shift the discussion. In acknowledging some merit to the other side's opinion, you are demonstrating to the undecideds that you're reasonable and open-minded. Bill Clinton displayed mastery of this technique in his debates with the first President Bush. Whenever Bush would make a statement, for instance on international affairs, Clinton would say, "Me too. I totally agree," and then he'd shift to the topic he wanted to discuss.

The trick is to find at least one detail of the opposition's argument that you agree with, acknowledge it, and then transition. It's similar to the strategy we talked about in Power #9, "Recognize Their Reality," where the manager was trying to persuade his staff to switch from Macs to PCs. The point is to demonstrate that you see your opponent's reality, because that builds trust. For example: "I agree with you, Tom, about the sick leave policy. No one should feel pressured to come to work when they're ill. Where we have a difference of opinion is on the definition of personal days." Remember that the undecideds have a hard time making up their minds because they see all sides of the issue, so you must prove to them that you can see all sides too.

If your opposition has some obvious strong points, acknowledging them right away will deflate the opposition a bit and also impress the undecideds. When Barack Obama was running against John McCain in 2008, he would begin every speech with the one truth all voters, including undecideds, agreed upon: "John McCain is a great American." Every speech, every town hall meeting, week after week, Obama opened his speeches with that line. Then he would move on to, "With that said . . . ," and explain all the ways he'd do things differently from McCain, after which he would characterize him as another George Bush.

One thing to keep in mind is that you don't need to win over all the undecideds, just enough to create a critical mass that's on your side. Once you have that, you can work on unifying the group, perhaps by making another concession or two to your opposition. You're not doing this to get the opposition to like you, but to demonstrate that you are practical and fair-minded. Your reasons for conceding a point must be strategic, not emotional.

A few undecideds will eventually get off the fence and choose sides. They will probably choose the person who treats them with the most respect and proves to be the most equitable. We see this all the time in mock juries, when jurors are choosing a foreman (they vote on the person). It's nearly always someone who has already voiced an opinion on the case. Jurors, including undecideds, are not looking for someone who is neutral. They're looking for a leader who will give everyone the opportunity to be heard. They're looking for a calm, measured person who can state both sides, focus on the important issues, make no reference to anyone's personal life, and make no value judgments about what someone else has said. That makes people feel secure. And those are exactly the same attributes that will win you the trust of undecideds no matter what group you're trying to persuade.

Undecided or Unaware? Project Implicit Wants to Know

During the 2008 presidential primary and election season, undecided voters bedeviled pollsters and, by the end of it all, infuriated millions of citizens. "Who are the undecideds?" asked writers, pundits, and prognosticators of every stripe. There were plenty of theories. *New York* magazine categorized some of the undecideds as "'low-information voters,' under-informed folks who tend to be older, less educated, and rural. Then there are those who are passionate about issues, but have been shaken loose of old voting habits."[1] According to "Moms for McCain," the undecideds were first-time voters, baby boomers, disgruntled Hillary Clinton supporters, and Catholics.[2] One survey reported, "They don't like NASCAR . . . they drive domestic cars . . . they are split evenly between George Washington and Abraham Lincoln as to who was the greatest president."[3]

"What is wrong with these people?" fumed Reuters' Andrea Hopkins. "After more than a year of nonstop political campaigning . . . what more do voters possibly need to know to make up their minds?"[4] Writing in the *Los Angeles Times*, Ezra Klein summed up the widespread frustration with undecideds: "From a civic standpoint, few creatures are as contemptible."[5]

Underlying much of the irritation was a suspicion that undecided voters weren't really undecided at all—they just enjoyed getting a lot of attention or were racist and didn't want to admit it to the pollsters. Four years earlier, a study of undecided voters in the 2004 election had come to the conclusion that undecideds weren't as confused as they claimed to be. It found that 80 percent of voters who called themselves "undecided" one month prior to the election had ended up voting for the candidate they had rated more favorably at the time they were polled. They basically knew who they were going to vote for, they just didn't admit it.[6]

But why? A 2008 survey conducted by researchers in Canada and Italy offered another perspective. Rather than intentionally misleading pollsters, this survey suggested that many undecided voters had actually made up their minds, but "they do not know it yet."[7] According to the survey's authors, undecideds have biases they are not aware of—"implicit" biases—that determine their votes. The study tested thirty-three people in a small Italian town who claimed to be undecided about the expansion of a U.S. military base. A simple computer test asked the undecideds to respond to positive or negative words associated with the U.S. base, and it measured the responses in milliseconds. The test theorized that people would hesitate when asked to push keys that conflicted with their true feelings, such as "base" and "good" if they really thought the base was bad. And they did hesitate, if only by a hundred milliseconds. By measuring that hesitation, the survey authors were able to predict the undecideds' actual votes with about 70 percent accuracy.

Thirty-three people is hardly a significant sample, but 4.5 million is. That's how many people have been tested in the same way by Project Implicit, a huge international online study being run by researchers at Harvard University, the University of Washington, and the University of Virginia. It's a virtual laboratory where you can test your own implicit biases, and about fifteen thousand people do so each week. Over the seven years the project has been in operation, the researchers have observed that "implicit biases are pervasive. . . . [For example,] over 80% of web respondents show implicit negativity toward the elderly compared to the young. . . . Ordinary people, including the researchers who direct this project, are found to harbor negative associations in relation to various social groups (i.e., implicit biases) even while honestly (the researchers believe) reporting that they regard themselves as lacking these biases." The researchers cite more than two hundred scientific studies that have used a version of their test, and conclude that implicit biases can predict behavior. The level of implicit bias varies from person to person, and it can be modified by experience.[8] If you're curious about your own implicit biases, you can test yourself at https://implicit.harvard.edu/implicit.

There seems to be good reason to assume that many undecideds are not aware of their own predispositions. I've certainly seen this in focus groups and mock juries. That's why I push so hard to uncover participants' core beliefs, and why I advise attorneys never to argue against a jury's predispositions. The good news is that among the undecideds, there are probably people who are already on your side.

POWER #19

Avoid Absolutes and Hypotheticals

I'd like to tell you never to use absolutes, but that would be an absolute, so I can't. With that said, avoid absolutes whenever possible, and don't answer hypotheticals. They are two versions of the same mistake: making a promise you might not be able to keep. Absolutes are statements that include words such as *all*, *always*, *never*, and the prefix *every*—*everyone*, *everything*, *everywhere*. Hypotheticals are the "What if?" questions reporters are always asking politicians: "What if your daughter were impregnated by a rapist—would you allow her to get an abortion?" "What if there were a ticking time bomb—would you torture a terrorist for information?"

In terms of persuasion, it's important to beware of absolutes because they're so tempting when you're making a pitch. If a prospect complains about people not returning phone calls, it's all too easy to reply, "We return every call the same day." There are two main reasons not to do this. One, it sounds unbelievable, which makes you seem untrustworthy; and two, it sets you up for failure. A third reason to avoid absolutes, especially in written form, is that they can get you into legal trouble.

The classic example of a political candidate being undone by an absolute was George H. W. Bush saying, "Read my lips: no new taxes." Bush's approval rating went from 90 percent in March 1991 to 37 percent in November 1992, when he lost the presidential election to Bill Clinton, a relatively unknown governor from a small Southern state. Bush's loss was largely attributed to that "No new taxes" promise, which he was unable to keep.

Why do politicians, and the rest of us, get trapped by absolutes? Because we want to seem strong and consistent. The truth is, it's a lot easier to be consistent if you haven't backed yourself into a corner with absolutes. So train yourself to remove them from your vocabulary unless you're talking about the past. For instance, while you should not say, "We will never miss a deadline," you can definitely say, "We have never yet missed a deadline, and our goal is to maintain that track record." It's always a good idea to mention past achievements and to say that you *plan* on keeping up the good work. Just remember not to exaggerate your accomplishments. People can and will check them online.

As for present or future declarations, replace absolutes with words that say basically the same thing but allow a little wiggle room. Often you can solve the problem by simply eliminating the absolute from your phrasing. Instead of saying, "All our customers love the product," say, "Our customers love the product." If you're answering a question that requires a quantity, such as "How often do customers complain about your hours?" Don't say "Never," say "Rarely." Replace words such as *everyone* and *everywhere* with *anyone* and *anywhere.*

Dealing with hypothetical questions is a bit more challenging than avoiding absolutes. That's because hypothetical questions often seem to demand an absolute response. Politicians are constantly struggling with hypotheticals while their opponents wait in the wings, ready to label them "liar" and "flip-flopper" if they don't take a stand. You could argue that it's a politician's duty to let us know how he or she might respond to unlikely hypotheticals such as a flu epidemic, terrorist attack, or natural disaster. That's how we decide whether or not to vote for someone. For businesspeople, however, the stakes are different. It makes no sense to respond to every improbable scenario someone dreams up. If you're pitching a new account or promoting a new strategy, your focus should be on presenting your cause as persuasively and honestly as you can, and that usually means not answering hypotheticals.

Some politicians bluntly refuse to answer hypotheticals and immediately start repeating their talking points. That method doesn't fly in business settings, where it can come off as defensive or rigid. A better approach is to soften the phrasing: "None of us can predict the future, so I don't like to answer hypotheticals." Then you can pivot to a past situation, a plan for the future, or both. For instance, let's say someone asks, "What if your product doesn't meet the revised federal standards in time for the rollout?" You could reply, "No one can predict the future, but I will say that it's never happened before. We intend to stay in close contact with the federal agency in charge of the new standards so that we're on top of any new deadlines." The basic formula is to decline to answer the hypothetical and then switch to something that is true (if in the past) or reasonable (if in the future). The overall effect is that you're honest and have given it some thought. That leaves a much better impression than a knee-jerk "We will meet every federal requirement," which is practically an invitation for the doubters in the crowd to prove you wrong.

Occasionally you may be asked a hypothetical question in a job interview. It's unnerving and can feel like a trap, but obviously you can't tell the interviewer that you don't like to answer hypotheticals. Luckily, the same approach outlined above also works here. Refer to something you have done successfully in the past that is relevant, then pivot to what you would *plan* on doing in the hypothetical situation, all the while avoiding absolutes. For instance:

INTERVIEWER: What if you found out on a Wednesday that all the reports had to be updated by Monday, and you had already promised two people vacation time?

APPLICANT: When I was at my last job, we did run into vacation conflicts every now and then, and I found that the relationships I had built with the staff really helped us get through the crunch. I worked hard to keep those relationships solid so I could call in favors when I needed to, and that's what I plan on doing if I work here.

In a job interview, as in all conversations, the other person will probably be using language that offers clues to the type of response that person wants to hear. Answering a hypothetical question can be a great opportunity to show your interviewer that you recognize his or her reality and that your goals are aligned. You can even try to use some of the interviewer's words or terms to create a subtle bond. If you need to spend a few moments pondering your response so you can connect all these dots, go ahead. As I'll explain in Power #20, people interpret silence as intelligence, which can only help you in a job interview. While you're thinking, cast your eyes down, not up. We've found from focus groups that looking up makes it seem as if you're searching for an answer, while looking down makes you appear serious and thoughtful. (See Power #27 for more presentation tips.)

Smackdown '88: Michael Dukakis

Just as George H. W. Bush was brought down by an absolute, his rival four years earlier had been destroyed by a hypothetical. Political junkies and others old enough to remember the 1988 election season will recall the famous debate between

Bush and Massachusetts governor Michael Dukakis that was moderated by CNN anchor Bernard Shaw. According to writer Roger Simon, "Shaw liked to see the candidates sweat. He liked to see the panic in their eyes." Simon quoted Shaw as saying that the election process was too easy on politicians: "They fly up and down the country asking for votes, and they ought to be forced to stand up and say what they really feel. Otherwise the voters are being jilted."[1]

Shaw was the moderator for the debate, so he was allowed only one question for each candidate before handing the floor over to a panel of news reporters. The question for Bush referenced his young, relatively inexperienced running mate, Dan Quayle: "If you are elected and die before inauguration day, automatically Dan Quayle would become the forty-first president of the United States. What have you to say about that possibility?" Unkind, perhaps, but it was nothing compared to the zinger Shaw aimed at Dukakis referencing the governor's wife, Kitty, and his opposition to the death penalty: "Governor, if Kitty Dukakis were raped and murdered, would you favor an irrevocable death penalty for the killer?"

The question remains one of the most controversial ever asked at a debate. Dukakis answered it coolly: "No, I don't, Bernard. And I think you know that I've opposed the death penalty during all of my life. I don't see any evidence that it's a deterrent, and I think there are better and more effective ways to deal with violent crime."[2]

This mild response undid Dukakis' candidacy. He was accused of being cold and unemotional, of basing his answer on principle rather than passion. The irony was that Michael Dukakis' principles had already been tested in real life. His elderly father had been the victim of a brutal beating during a robbery, and his brother had been killed by a hit-and-run driver. Dukakis remained a steadfast opponent of the death penalty despite these tragedies. His handlers had even prepared an "emotional" response to crime questions in which Dukakis was supposed to mention all that. But Shaw's question, right out of the starting gate, took Dukakis by surprise. He answered the hypothetical without stopping to think, and it earned him a reputation for being hard-hearted that helped lose him the election.

Ten years later, in 1998, master communicator Bill Clinton was not about to fall for a similar trap. On the ropes during the Monica Lewinsky scandal, Clinton repeatedly declined to answer questions about his relationship with Lewinsky because of the ongoing legal investigation. At one press conference, CNN's Wolf Blitzer decided to take a more personal tack: "Mr. President, Monica Lewinsky's life has been changed forever. Her family's life has been changed forever. I wonder how you feel about that, and what, if anything, you'd like to say to Monica Lewinsky at this minute." It wasn't exactly a hypothetical question, but almost.

"That's good," Clinton responded, as if to give Blitzer props for his tactic. The president let a few seconds pass, then repeated, "That's good. But I think at this minute I'm going to stick to my position and not comment."

Blitzer later said, "He almost bit. For several seconds there he paused, and I could see he was almost ready to say something. . . . He's told us what didn't happen, but he's never told us what kind of relationship he did have with Monica Lewinsky. I wanted to elicit some reaction from him. Close, but no cigar."[3]

POWER #20

Learn How to Use Silence

All the great communication experts use silence to persuade. Salespeople, journalists, and politicians are especially good at it. In fact, there's an excellent chance you have already experienced silence as a sales tool. Ever buy a car at a dealership? The typical scenario is that you've selected the car and now you're seated across the desk from the salesman. He waits. You make an offer, trying to sound as macho and confident as you can. He listens to your offer, shakes his head a little, frowns slightly, and says nothing. The minutes tick by until you finally blurt out something like, "I could *maybe* go a little bit higher." It's the classic negotiator's ploy: the first one to speak loses. Unless you're a skilled negotiator yourself, you have little chance of waiting him out, because the silence becomes unbearable. He has just used silence to persuade you to raise your own offer.

Reporters use silence to draw information from interview subjects. They'll smile, nod, go "Mm-hmmm" a lot, and if the other person stops talking, they'll nod again and say nothing for a few more seconds until the interviewee feels compelled to start talking again. Veteran journalist Bob Dotson has described how he uses silence to get the most memorable quotes: "People nearly always answer questions in three parts. First they tell you what they think you've asked. Then, they explain in more detail. If you don't jump right in with another question, if you let the silence between you build, they figure you don't yet understand and make an extra effort to explain their thoughts more concisely. Often, they make their point more passionately and precisely the third time."[1]

When I'm conducting focus groups, I do a version of the same thing. I keep asking, "Why?" in order to get to the core beliefs of the participants, and if people don't answer, I don't speak until they do. (Remember that in order to persuade, you need to understand other people's perspective so you can align your reality with theirs. That's why it's so important to know what their core beliefs are.) In a business setting, you can use Dotson's strategy by asking a question and waiting long enough to hear all three parts of the answer, perhaps nudging the person along with a "Hmmm," or "Really?" and then staying quiet.

As a political consultant, I frequently coach my clients on when *not* to respond to a reporter's questions. Politicians love to talk, so this is a crucial survival skill they need to develop. "They can't print it out of context if you never say it in the first place," I tell them. Tolerating a reporter's silence also helps the politician figure out how good a journalist he or she is dealing with, because the best reporters can wait out anyone, no matter how rich, famous, or powerful.

Experienced politicians are also skilled at using silence. Thanks to YouTube, you can watch them in action. Observe the way Bill Clinton pauses and ponders his reply in order to make a reporter feel as if he has just asked an unexpected, thought-provoking question. (Do you really think there are many questions Clinton doesn't anticipate?) You can use the same technique when making a presentation to a group. If you know what the objections are likely to be and have already developed answers for them, the strategy is simple. Listen to the objection, wait a few beats, ponder it, and then say, "So you're saying that if we do X, Y could be the result. Good point." Wait another beat or two. "What if we handled it like this?" You have recognized the person's reality, boosted his or her ego, and dealt with the objection.

Silence is useful in other ways too. If someone is dominating a discussion, let the person finish a sentence, then wait a few moments before you respond. It puts you back in control. (No matter how you feel about the people in the room, always let them finish their sentences. If you cut them off, it will seem as if you don't care about what they have to say or haven't been listening. Since the ultimate goal is to soothe egos and unify the room, you don't want to insult anyone.)

Once you're aware of the power of silence, you will see how often it can be used to your advantage. If someone attacks you or your idea, simply let the person's words hang in the air for a few moments before you respond. Silence always feels longer to the person who is speaking, so that person will already be squirming a little by the time you talk. If you're making a sales call, rather than bombarding the customer with every detail, leave plenty of spaces for the customer to fill in with a comment or question. That's what gets the customer invested in the process. Finally, being comfortable with silence signals that you're comfortable with yourself. Whether you're walking down a hall with a colleague or flying across the country with him, he will be calmed and reassured by comfortable silence. It's a lot easier to live with than nonstop chatter.

The other side of understanding silence is knowing how to interpret it. Every so often I'll wrap up a presentation and the only sound will be the hum of the air conditioner. I'll say, "Judging by the silence, I must have covered this topic brilliantly," which usually gets a laugh. The natural tendency is to panic and assume that your audience hasn't understood the presentation or hasn't liked it, or that you have somehow failed. That's not how you want to feel when you're trying to persuade a group. Where does the truth lie? It could be that they didn't understand you, that they don't agree with you, or that you actually did cover it brilliantly. Don't assume that the silence is a bad sign and don't take it personally.

It seems to be a human inclination to confuse silence with intelligence or wisdom. I learned that the hard way. Silence is such a powerful force that I once hired a man who was relatively mute during his job interview. He conversed a little bit, he looked presentable, and he smiled and nodded knowingly to all my comments, so I assumed he was intelligent. I found out later he was nodding because he didn't have a clue what I was talking about.

I've thought about that interview many times, because if

anyone should have been alert to the possibilities of silence, it was me. Yet because of my ego—he nodded and smiled and generally boosted mine—I forgot to actually listen to him. The experience reminded me that whenever I'm not sure what to say, I should probably keep quiet. People will assume I'm intelligent unless I prove them wrong.

POWER #21

Get Physical

Touch, beginning with but not limited to the handshake, can be a valuable tool in persuasion. The obvious experts are politicians, whose moves can be studied for hours via the Internet. Bill Clinton and Lyndon Johnson represent the extremes of using touch and physical presence to unify people or, in Johnson's case, intimidate them. Either method can help you persuade—by now I'm sure you know which one I prefer.

Bill Clinton famously loved pressing the flesh. Merely by placing his hand lightly at the small of a woman's back, he could make her feel as if she were the only person in the room.

He was equally appealing to men, even those who wanted to resist. On *Dennis Miller Live* in June 2000, Jon Stewart described meeting the then-president. It was apparently quite a physical experience: "He's the most incredibly charismatic bullshit artist. . . . He healed me! I was blind, he touched me, I can see. [He's] your height when he talks to you. He was five-seven for me, for my mom he was five feet tall. . . . He just envelops you in this tasty goodness. . . . It's crazy. He's good."[1] Here's a photo of Clinton still at it in 2008, "enveloping" New Mexico Lieutenant Governor Diane Denish:

Mark G. Bralley

When guys like Bill Clinton meet you, they'll pull your hand in to touch their chest or their stomach, or they'll put

two hands on your hand. They pull you all the way in because when you're not afraid to touch or be close, people like you more.

Lyndon Johnson, in contrast, used his height (he was nearly six-four) to overpower opponents—the press called it the Johnson Treatment. Below he is seen in 1965, practicing the art of persuasion with Associate Supreme Court Justice Abe Fortas:

Yoichi R. Okamoto/LBJ Library

He could do it to a group too. On the next page, he is seen speaking with members of Congress:

Yoichi R. Okamoto/LBJ Library

In *Master of the Senate*, author Robert A. Caro quotes journalists Rowland Evans and Robert Novak describing the Johnson Treatment: "The Treatment could last ten minutes or four hours. . . . He moved in close, his face a scant millimeter from his target, his eyes widening and narrowing, his eyebrows rising and falling. . . . Mimicry, humor, and the genius of analogy made The Treatment an almost hypnotic experience and rendered the target stunned and helpless." That's much closer to coercion than persuasion, and I don't recommend it, but it's a fascinating example of how physical presence can affect an audience.

In the current White House, Michelle Obama seems to be the one with the magic touch. Barack uses all the standard power moves—grasp the arm, pull the other person in, offer a manly hug. Michelle gets more personal. A woman who met the First Lady at a luncheon described how Michelle touched her shoulder, then moved her hand up to lightly touch her hair. After that, "I would have done anything for her," she said.

Your own use of touch has to be something that you are comfortable with and that is socially appropriate. At work, you need to be careful not to cross any lines that the opposite sex might find either offensive or distracting. That said, there are many studies showing that the human touch eases anxiety, slows the heart rate, and drops blood pressure in the person being touched. The healing power of touch is a real phenomenon, and you can use it to put colleagues at ease.

It's usually acceptable to touch a colleague on the hand, forearm, shoulder, or upper back. In one-on-one conversations, touching the other person's arm or hand will instantly make that person stop talking. You can do it to subtly get the other person to be quiet if he or she is talking too much, or to get the other person to stay quiet while you're making a point. In general, the person who initiates the touching is asserting power. If you're dealing with a superior whom you don't want to challenge, you probably shouldn't touch him or her beyond the initial handshake. If you're in the superior position, use touch to establish a bond—a brief pat on the back or shoulder is fine. You don't need to touch someone a lot in order to establish that you're open to friendship. One light touch on the arm while you're making a point is all it takes.

POWER #22

Don't Say No, Say "Let's Try This"

"Never say no" is one of those sales credos that makes people's blood pressure shoot up. The implication is that you've got to say yes to everything and then have a heart attack trying to meet impossible demands. Yet when you're dealing with clients, you really can't say no if you want to keep the business. You must satisfy them and at the same time persuade them not to pursue ideas that would be bad for their cause.

My team frequently uses this tactic when we're working with corporations involved in lawsuits. One common scenario is that we get called in as crisis consultants when the

CEO is feeling besieged by all the bad publicity a lawsuit is generating. The first thing out of the CEO's mouth is usually "I want you to send out a press release," and the press release is supposed to tell the company's side of the story. Unfortunately, that isn't newsworthy. Worse, if it does make it into the papers, it might make the company look desperate.

But CEOs don't like to hear the word *no* any more than the rest of us do. No is a rejection. Say no, and you've just made your client feel stupid. You've also given the impression that you don't care about your client's goal. Instead of saying no, take the conversation back to the goal and suggest alternate ways to achieve it.

For instance, with the panicky CEOs, I usually ask, "You want to generate some positive publicity to counter the lawsuit news, is that right? Because your basic goal is to show the public that you're an ethical company." Then I start suggesting third-party validators who can supply that good press: "You don't always want to respond directly to charges. Sometimes it's more effective if other credible people tell the story for you. What about your satisfied customers? What about that foundation you support? Could someone write an article for the newspaper focusing on a charity event you spearheaded? What about cashing in on all that goodwill you've built in your twenty years of service to this community?"

Now the client is excited. I haven't shot down his or her idea about a press release; instead, I've added more ideas to it. I've expanded ways to reach the client's goal. If you keep the goal as your touchstone, you'll have safe common ground you can return to. From that place of unity, you can change the process together.

Many times, the thing people are asking for is not what they really want. They come to you talking about a specific process, and what they really want is to accomplish a certain goal. Suppose your brother announces, "I want everyone in the family to come to our house this Thanksgiving." Instead of saying, "No, we can't. We hate to travel then," you might try to get a sense of his underlying goal: "Is there a particular reason you want everyone at your place?" Maybe what he really wants is for the whole family to see his newly renovated kitchen. Maybe that can happen sometime other than Thanksgiving. Or maybe what he's craving is a family reunion, and it doesn't need to be at his house or at Thanksgiving, as long as it happens soon. If you take it back to the goal, the answer is rarely no, it's usually "Let's accomplish it this way."

Earlier in this book, I advised you not to ignore bad news. It's just as critical that you find a positive way to say no, as contradictory as that may seem. In personal or business relationships, people in our culture are drawn to optimists. Especially in the workplace, being positive is strongly encouraged. All too often, people who deliver bad news are reprimanded, as I was when I slipped all those "negative" clippings under the legislators' doors in my first political job. Saying no is frequently seen as just being negative. Saying "Let's try this" instead is not only an important part of persuasion, it's a valuable survival tool in any business environment.

Even the little things count when you're trying to present a generally positive face to the world. Before you hit the send button on your emails, reread them and try to eliminate the word *no* whenever you (reasonably) can. It usually takes only a few seconds to rephrase the message in a positive way.

POWER #23

Release Bad News Quickly and Good News Slowly

A large part of persuasion has to do with how you manage facts, especially when the facts could damage your reputation. There's a classic battle between lawyers and public relations people over this issue. The folks in PR understand that the longer a story drags out, the worse it is for whoever is at the eye of the storm. Lawyers, meanwhile, want to release bad news in little pieces and as infrequently as possible. They have their legal reasons, but they don't realize that perception drives attitudes, even with something as serious as a lawsuit. If you can get all the details of a bad story out in one day, there's a good chance it will blow over because there will be nothing for the media to follow up with. That, in turn, will influence the perception of every citizen who hears about the case, including potential jurors.

Assessing juror attitudes has been my business for a long time now, and all my experience leads to the same conclusion, which is that perception creates reality. The Enron case stands out as a good example, because there was a lot of discussion in the media about whether Ken Lay, Jeffrey Skilling, and the other Enron execs could get a fair trial in Houston, where the company was headquartered. I recall reading an interview with a prospective juror and a couple of citizens, each of whom insisted that *of course* the Enron guys could get a fair trial in Houston, and by the way, they needed to go to jail. If a judge had asked them, "Can you forget that thousands of Enron employees lost their retirement savings?" I'm sure the jurors would have said, "Yes, I can be fair. I can only look at the facts." And they would have meant it—people fool themselves into thinking they can forget their perceptions. But they can't. No one can. That's why it's crucial to understand how to release the facts in a way that will create the perception that supports your position.

The most excruciating and damaging example of releasing bad news too slowly was the Monica Lewinsky scandal. Remember how long it dragged out, how the details came out bit by bit, month after month? The internal battle must have been fierce, with the lawyers saying "Don't release this!" and the PR folks begging President Clinton to just get it all out there at once, because then it's a one-day story. Ten semi-bad stories are much more damaging than one really bad story that includes the same ten details.

The reverse is also true: If you've got good news, release it slowly and as piecemeal as you can, because the cumulative effect is much more powerful. Let's say a candidate gets an endorsement from the AFL-CIO, which has sixty-five member unions. If you release the news in one day, even if you say there are sixty-five members and list all of them, the story remains a one-day story. But if you release one union endorsement every four days for the next twenty-three weeks, the perception is that everybody's supporting this guy. You create the reality because you've managed the perception.

It works like this in every area of life, and the knowledge is especially useful in business. In terms of bad news, consider how your employees would react if you told them all the negatives at once: This year you're going to have to forgo raises, and there will be no bonuses, and there's also going to be a 10 percent staff cut. That's a brutal message to deliver, and people won't be happy. Now imagine if you delivered one of those messages every week for three weeks. The staff would be worse than unhappy, they'd be in a panic wondering what disaster was awaiting them at the next meeting. The same rules apply if you're a staff member and have to tell your supervisor bad news. Spill the entire story at once, and it's one bad day. Stretch it over days or weeks, and it looks like you don't know how to do your job.

It works in reverse for good news at work just as in campaigns. If there's a way to release positive client feedback slowly, the effect will be greater and the glow will last longer. It's counterintuitive, because we all have a natural tendency to spread good news the minute we hear it and to minimize bad news. If we can learn to do the opposite, we can have more control over the way the people around us perceive the facts.

Crisis Control for Beginners

Crisis control experts are public relations people who work behind the scenes to help individuals or organizations manage serious threats to their reputation or business. Their mission is to resolve sensitive situations, to influence public opinion, and to create a perception of their client that is more favorable, or at least less unfavorable. If a crisis is handled well, it quickly fades from public consciousness. Naturally, the parties involved want it to stay that way. That's why crisis experts are a little bit secretive about their clients. My firm has done its share of crisis control, and I'm aware of the challenges. I wanted to talk to someone who specializes exclusively in this field, so I contacted one of Southern California's most experienced crisis consultants, Roger Gillott, the founder of Gillott Communications, and asked if I could interview him. He said sure, as long as I didn't use the names of his clients. His insights are valuable, so I agreed.

"When it comes to crisis control, there are three basic rules," Gillott told me. "First, you need to control the situation and not let it control you. Second, you must engage the media, because if you don't tell your story, the other side will tell it for you, and you're not going to like the way it turns out. Third, whenever you do deal with the media, you've absolutely got to get it right the first time, because there are no do-overs."

"Release bad news quickly" is an approach he follows in most crisis situations, from corporate bankruptcies to prominent individuals who get busted for drugs or other indiscretions. A one-day story is far more desirable than one that drags on—and drags the client's reputation down—for weeks or months. Hedging your bets and releasing bad news slowly usually backfires, he believes. "The best recent example is the financial crisis, where a bank would say, 'We're going to write off a billion dollars this quarter, and that should resolve this problem.' Next quarter, they write off another two billion. Better to just take a bigger worst-case write-off at the outset and get it over with. It's like laying off employees. Don't do it by dribs and drabs. Morale just goes through the floor. If it's bad news, get it done fast and get it behind you."

Gillott defines his work as crisis management and reputation management. "Every crisis affects your reputation," he explains. "Not every reputation issue is necessarily a crisis. But they're all sensitive issues, and they're all critical to the client. I've met with potential clients who are in denial—they don't want to admit they're in a crisis. But if you say, 'This is an issue that's going to affect your reputation,' they have no trouble with that. Go figure."

In crisis control, your sparring partner is usually the media because that's your conduit to the public. Gillott recalled a situation where his client was under criminal investigation by the IRS. "He was the president of a nonprofit organization. The people who planted the seeds with the IRS also leaked it to a major newspaper. Soon a reporter came snooping around. What the client hoped for, in his heart of hearts, was to avoid a story entirely. I told him up front that this most likely was not going to happen, given that the reporter was already on to it."

Yet Gillott was ultimately able to sidetrack the story. "I took three tacks. The first was to discredit the people who had planted the allegations with the IRS and leaked them to the paper. The second was to convince the reporter that it was not a competitive story and that, should any other news organization start inquiring about it, my first call would be to alert the initial reporter. I was confident that the story was not going to be competitive. But even if it had been, I would have kept the promise. The reporter knew me and knew that. The third tack was to convince the reporter that this IRS investigation was all smoke, but if something did come of it, my client would cooperate with him a hundred percent."

What about stonewalling? "Going silent is a terrible idea, because if you say nothing you abdicate your opportunity to influence the story. Saying too much isn't helpful either, because if you stir a lot of dirt in the air all you're doing is obscuring your message. The best response is 'Let me check on that and I'll get back to you.' That buys you time to refine the message and polish the tone and language so it's just right. But you've absolutely got to get back to that reporter and you've got to do so before his deadline. If you don't, you've broken a promise and the reporter is never going to trust you in the future."

In a sensitive situation, Gillott told me, the single most important thing to remember when dealing with the media is "Never let them see you sweat. You can't betray the slightest tinge of nervousness and you can't lose your cool. If the media ever sees you wavering, they will pound on you mercilessly and you'll never get off the defensive."

Gillott worked for the Associated Press for twelve years and was one of its more highly regarded reporters nationwide. "I know how reporters think," he said. "They show no mercy, and what they want most of all is a prominent byline, a prominent spot on the six o'clock news, or the most hits on a website. Which is why the best person to handle PR in sensitive situations is usually someone who was a reporter in an earlier life. He knows all the tricks because he's used them himself."

In short, what should a potential client look for in evaluating a crisis control expert? "Someone who handles stress well and doesn't lose composure. Someone who's been around the block often and exudes command presence. And an adrenaline junkie who revels in going eyeball-to-eyeball with the media—and doesn't blink."

POWER #24

Challenge Bad Ideas by Challenging the Details

Not every persuasion campaign is about urging people to do something. Occasionally you need to persuade them *not* to do something you think is a bad idea. The most effective method is to agree with the larger concept, then challenge the details. (There is always some level at which you can agree on the concept, as I'll explain in a moment.) You're already familiar with this tactic if you pay any attention to political ads. The formula is to have either an expert or an average citizen saying, "We all want X. But the Z Act isn't the way to do it. Z will . . ." Fill in the blank: "limit our choices" . . . "take away our rights" . . . "fail to hold people accountable" . . . "raise our taxes" . . . "provide no oversight," and so forth. These ads are either incredibly irritating or outstanding, depending on your feelings about the issue. But they work. That's why you keep seeing them.

A classic example was a campaign funded by the tobacco industry to defeat Proposition 86, which in 2006 sought to raise the tobacco tax in California. The anti–Prop. 86 television commercial featured a physician. Here's the script:

> I'm Dr. Mark Kogan. Like any doctor, I do everything in my power to convince people to stop smoking. But that's not what Prop. 86 is all about. Prop. 86 raises billions in taxes but dedicates only ten percent to anti-smoking programs. The rest of the money goes to special interests sponsoring the measure and to more government bureaucracy. Read for yourself. Prop. 86 is not what it claims. That's why doctors, police, business, and taxpayer protection groups oppose Prop. 86.[1]

Talk about hitting all the marks. You have an expert advocate agreeing with the concept, then decimating the details. He uses numbers: the "billions" the tax will collect, out of which a mere "ten percent" will be spent on anti-smoking programs. Cue the emotional language: "Special interests" and "government bureaucracy" will reap most of the billions. For good measure, other third-party advocates are added to the pitch—the "doctors, police, business, and taxpayer protection groups" who oppose the tax. Proposition 86 narrowly failed to pass, so the strategy was successful.

You may loathe tobacco or love it, but the point is that this method works. It works anywhere, and knowing how to use it can come in very handy. Basically, the approach is the opposite of unifying people around a goal. When you're trying to persuade people to do something, you want them to focus on the goal, the grand mission that you all agree on, and not get distracted by the process. When you want to persuade people *not* to do something, you need to agree with the goal but then quickly focus their attention on flaws in the process. You never outright oppose the goal, and you try not to use negatives when countering the bad idea.

When challenging bad ideas in the workplace, your first task is to identify the big-picture concept that you agree with. Let's say one of your supervisors wants to guarantee that every workweek is capped at forty hours. You can't do that, because it would make your business less competitive during rush seasons. To find agreement, you must make the concept bigger: You can agree that all employees need downtime. You can agree that you value your employees, and that they all need time to recharge their batteries. But that doesn't mean (here come the details) that everybody needs this specific amount of time off. You can say, "I agree that everyone needs downtime. The problem with a forty-hour week, specifically, is that there are weeks when we need to work five ten-hour days, because rush orders come in and we have to fill them. So what we need is two full weeks off around Christmas, so that everyone can get away from the job completely. In the end, our employees will get as much downtime as anyone, but I think limiting every workweek to forty hours is a mistake and could hurt this company." You took it to the larger goal, agreed with it, and then talked about how the specifics would not accomplish that larger goal. And you offered a legitimate alternative, which is always the best approach if you can manage it.

Gerrymandering and "Old White Judges"

For decades, California's electoral districts were so unfairly manipulated (gerrymandered) that both Democrats and Republicans were deeply entrenched in their respective areas. The candidates who got elected tended to represent the more extreme ends of each party—conservative Republicans on the one hand and ultraliberal Democrats on the other. Neither side could compromise with the other for fear of infuriating their core constituents. As a result, the state government was gridlocked, unable to resolve California's serious financial troubles. Five times over twenty-six years, bills were introduced that would redraw the districts in a more equitable fashion. Each time, the opposition ran ads damning the details. They succeeded the first four times.

Then, in 2008, California finally passed a statewide redistricting bill. Proposition 11 was backed by both Democrats and Republicans, and prior to the election my firm was hired to conduct focus groups and help develop an ad campaign that would trump the inevitable opposition.

To prepare, we looked at the ads for Proposition 77, the most recent failed attempt. According to the League of Women Voters, a *yes* vote on Prop. 77 meant that "boundaries for political districts would be drawn by retired judges and approved by voters at statewide elections." A *no* vote meant the boundaries would continue to be drawn by the legislature and approved by the governor.[2]

One of the most famous "Yes on 77" television commercials featured a cane-wielding senior citizen (really an actress) hobbling down the walkway to her front door, muttering,

"Legislature, ha, ha. . . . They rig the election; they rig everything. And what do you get for it? Nothing. All they do is money, money, money." A voice-over intoned, "Legislators draw their own districts, so they can't lose. . . . Proposition 77 has independent judges draw district lines, not the politicians."

The opposing "No on 77" campaign turned the "retired independent judges" into the damning details. The *L.A. Times* reported that, "One no-on-77 television spot shows three men in black robes who are clearly up to no good. They furiously cut apart a map of California and then work, grimacing, at putting the pieces back together. As they do, the announcer warns that the measure would change the state Constitution 'just for political gain.'"[3] The message was that old white men, in cahoots with Governor Arnold Schwarzenegger, would be carving up the districts to the detriment of everyone in the state who was not old, white, and male. The League of Women Voters' Trudy Schafer delivered a textbook "kill it with the details" statement to the press: "We do want to see reform in how district lines are drawn, but we think there are too many flaws in Prop. 77."[4]

The people who hired me to research Prop. 11 knew that getting retired judges to draw the districts would be dead in the water. They instructed me to ask the focus groups what they thought of a redistricting commission made up of fourteen "average citizens." What did we learn? No one thought Prop. 11 was going to fix politics. No one thought they were ever going to change the mind-set of politicians, who were really just in it for themselves, or that they were going to rein in special interests. And no one thought that the "average citizens" in the commission would be completely immune to political pressure. But they kept coming back to "It's something. It gives me a little more control because there won't be old white judges this time."

Prop. 11 was framed as a reform issue and focused on the fourteen-citizen commission. Sure enough, its opponents tried to kill it with a campaign that was all about the confusing details. A signature "No on 11" television ad did not oppose the concept of redistricting. It argued, once again, that this wasn't the right way to go about it. A silver-haired professorial gent stood before a large hand-drawn flowchart, using a pointer to explain Prop. 11 to an indignant sixty-something woman:

MAN: "Prop. 11. Bureaucrats choose sixty candidates for a fourteen-member Redistricting Commission. Legislative leaders have their veto. Then eight of the fourteen are selected by a random draw and those eight get to pick the other six. . . .

VOICE-OVER: "No on Prop. 11—too confusing, too complicated, and totally unfair."

Meanwhile, "Yes on Prop. 11" groups aired a commercial that pitted the "politicians" who were opposed to Prop. 11 against the many organizations that were for it. In the ad, an attractive young woman strode onto a sleek, modern set and computer graphics materialized in the air next to her to illustrate her points. It was a stark contrast to the seniors featured in the "No on 11" ad. The "Yes on 11" commercial included no information other than the proposition's goal and a list of third-party validators:

WOMAN: You can tell a lot about a proposition by who is sponsoring it. Prop. 11 is opposed by the politicians, but sponsored by the League of Women Voters, AARP, the California Taxpayers Association, and the list goes on. The politicians say no to 11. The League of Women Voters and all these folks say Prop. 11 makes it easier to vote politicians out of office if they don't do their jobs. You know what side your friends are on. Yes on 11.[5]

In fact, some powerful politicians, including Governor Schwarzenegger, did support Prop. 11 and were openly campaigning for it. They were not mentioned in the "Yes" ad, but in the end this bit of dodging didn't matter. The third-party validators and the citizens' commission were enough to overcome assaults on Prop. 11's details, and it passed.

This is an important lesson to remember when someone is trying to kill *your* idea with details. Don't get drawn into the argument, because what is there to say? They think the details are flawed (or that's the position they're taking) and you do not. Rather than squabble, briefly agree to disagree, then transition back to the goal and point to all the credible third-party advocates who support you.

POWER #25

Play Devil's Advocate

As we saw in the last chapter, challenging a bad idea by challenging the details is a strategy for completely halting a dubious plan. Playing devil's advocate is a different technique, one that can be used either to deflate someone else's proposal or to locate weaknesses in your own idea.

Why would you want to find weaknesses in your plan? For the same reason my attorney clients want me to pinpoint holes in their legal arguments: Fixing those flaws makes the argument stronger. Some CEOs will actually assign a devil's advocate during meetings, so that at least one person feels free to express the "negative" viewpoint that so often gets stifled in the workplace, especially when top management is in the room.

Whenever you present a plan, there's a chance someone will voice doubts. Instead of getting defensive, you can say, "That's a fair point. Want to play devil's advocate? We can try to get a handle on potential problems sooner rather than later." Now you're all on the same side, and the doubter has a specific role in the discussion. This isn't intended to placate people—understanding the weaknesses in your plan really is just as important as understanding the strengths. As a nice side benefit, asking someone to play devil's advocate will show the undecideds in the room that you're open-minded, which will help sway them in your direction.

Knowing how to play devil's advocate is also crucial when defending various aspects of your plan against people who want to alter it. Let's say you're trying to persuade the greeting card company where you work to launch a new line of cards. You know that the soonest the line can be ready is Mother's Day, but that will bypass Valentine's Day, the second biggest card-giving holiday of the year. You assume the boss will try to accelerate the line's production. The best way to counter his idea is to begin by saying something positive about it: "I agree that a Valentine's Day launch would be ideal.

But can I play devil's advocate for a minute? If we promise the new line by Valentine's Day and only a few designs are ready by then, it could undermine retailers' perception of the entire line."

Playing devil's advocate is solution-driven and direct. Nuance is not the way to go when you need to voice uncomfortable or unpopular topics. You have to be straightforward. It's fine to say something discreet one time ("Are you concerned about . . . ?"), but you'll come off as nagging or paranoid if you keep asking, "Are you concerned about . . . ?" "Aren't you worried about . . . ?" "What if X happened?" By playing devil's advocate, you're getting it out in the open and letting everyone know exactly what your concerns are.

When I'm playing devil's advocate, one phrase I try to avoid is "I don't disagree with you, but . . ." As soon as other people hear that, they'll be on the defensive. What they hear is, "I disagree with you. Brace yourself for my criticism." You've moved away from finding a solution, and instead you're setting up a conflict. It's much more productive to say, "Is it okay if I play devil's advocate? I want to anticipate any snags. Whatever disagreements we have will only help us create a more airtight strategy." Now you've taken it back to a problem-solving exercise, and any time the tension starts rising, you can say, "Remember, I'm just playing devil's advocate so we're sure we have every angle covered." You're always trying to get the most positive feeling happening in the room, and you're always aiming to make people feel comfortable and safe.

It's not unusual for participants in my focus groups to get combative with me, because I often need to keep questioning them (even provoking them) until I get to the core of how they really feel. In these groups, playing devil's advocate is how I take the edge off the argument. It reminds them that I'm literally playing a role so that I can understand them better. They usually start repeating it to one another—"He's just playing devil's advocate"—because I argue both sides pretty passionately. For dealing with opponents, doubters, touchy issues, sensitive egos, or a room full of careful colleagues and an intimidating boss, playing devil's advocate works. That's why this simple term gets its own chapter.

POWER #26

Don't Change, "Adapt"

All political candidates know that during the course of a campaign, current events may force them to change their position on an important issue. That can spark an internal battle about how the message should change and how the change should be presented to voters. The same thing happens in business, and when it does, experienced leaders unify their group around the concept that good ideas evolve.

In a campaign, the reason a candidate has to change is usually pretty obvious. An event has occurred that grabs the public's attention, and the candidate ignores it at his or her peril. We saw it happen in 2008. When the showdown between Barack Obama and John McCain began, both candidates were focused on international affairs—Obama because his biggest calling card was his opposition to the Iraq War, and McCain because foreign affairs were his strong suit. But the Obama team was more attuned to the national mood, and they soon figured out that whoever found his voice on the economy first would win the election. Obama began to shift his message. When McCain would bring up homeland security or the war on terror, Obama would point out that the Iraq War had cost a lot of money and was a big factor in the economic downturn. The McCain camp was slow to understand that the conversation had changed, and that was a major reason John McCain lost.

When I worked as a political strategist and wrote campaign plans, I always tried to lay a good foundation for managing change, even though I couldn't know exactly what the change might be. As my team and I were brainstorming the plan, we'd make sure everybody in the campaign had a piece of the creative pie. We would run the concepts by not only the candidate but also the people on the finance committee and anyone else who was in on the ground floor, and we integrated their ideas as much as we could. It built unity and it was also strategic, because when a message needs to change, conflict can erupt between those who created the message and those who did not. The ones who created it are more likely to cling to the message and feel threatened by change. They may even be worried about losing their jobs. The ones who didn't contribute to the message may be tempted to point fingers or use the situation to gain leverage. But if everyone contributed to the original plan, there's a sense that "We're all in this together; no single one of us is to blame." Everyone will also feel more enthusiastic about creating and promoting an evolved message.

In business as well as politics, outside events are what usually forces change. It could be new technology, a turn in the economy, or a rival café that opens across the street from your café. If you're in charge, you need to persuade your team to follow you to the next stage and not panic or jump ship. You can do it using the same strategies we talked about at the beginning of this book. First, take everyone back to the founding goal of the organization. Then have the group help you decide how the message should evolve, while still supporting the original mission. When everyone has contributed, you will have the unity you need to start moving in the new direction. The key lies in giving ownership of the changed message to the group, and also in personally accepting responsibility for whatever problems there were with the original message or strategy. Share the credit and assume the blame—in other words, keep your ego out of it and make sure everyone else's ego is soothed and safe.

Where change gets more complicated in both politics and business is in presenting the new, evolved candidate or product to the voter or consumer. You may have spent years building a brand, and now all of a sudden it's different. With a politician, this can be a very perilous time. With a product or service, the trick is to make the new version seem like a natural evolution of the original. What often helps bridge the gap is one of the three reliable concepts—choice, fairness, and accountability. If you're offering one of those, change becomes much more appealing.

In 2009, Kentucky Fried Chicken (KFC) launched exactly this type of transformation. The fast-food chain had struggled for years to attract health-conscious customers, to no avail. In 2008 it had switched cooking oils and announced that its fried chicken now contained zero grams of fat, but sales in the United States still declined by 3 percent that year. It was impossible to persuade people that the brand with "fried" in its name was healthy. In the early 1990s, two attempts to introduce non-fried options—rotisserie-style and roast chicken—had failed.

In April 2009, KFC got its messaging and its product in

sync and tried again, this time with grilled chicken. What customers loved about the original KFC was the flavor—"11 secret herbs and spices." So Kentucky grilled chicken would also have a secret recipe, a combination of six herbs and spices. "For years, KFC has worked tirelessly to perfect a grilled option that has the great flavor and taste America associates with Colonel Sanders' Original recipe," their press release announced. "We're confident that KFC's second secret recipe, Kentucky Grilled Chicken, is one that the Colonel would have approved of."

The grilled chicken was priced the same as the fried chicken, and thanks to new grilling ovens, it cooked as quickly as the fried. It, too, was sold in buckets. Ad campaigns addressed the health issue head-on with the slogan "UNTHINK what you thought about KFC." For third-party credibility, television spots featured endorsements from celebrity chefs. The ultimate endorser, Oprah Winfrey, offered a coupon for a free two-piece chicken meal on her website, and she touted the offer on her show.

KFC's campaign touched all the important points in the "good ideas evolve" approach: making the change about choice, working directly off the original message (in this case, the original recipe), and making the new product similar enough to the original in look and delivery that it didn't seem as if KFC were abandoning its core comfort food–loving customers. In January 2010, KFC reported that the grilled chicken had racked up nearly $1 billion in sales its first year. David Novak, chief executive of KFC parent company Yum! Brands, declared, "Kentucky Grilled Chicken has been an unqualified success. We needed to broaden the appeal of this brand and we have done it."[1]

Starbucks' Growing Pains

Not even Starbucks is immune to the winds of change. In January 2008, as the world economy turned southward, Starbucks' stock began to fall. Founder and former CEO Howard Schultz was brought back to revitalize the brand. The result of his "Transformation Agenda" is not entirely clear as of this writing, but the way Schultz went about implementing change offers interesting food for thought.

The Starbucks brand had been built on the concept of paying premium prices for an exceptional coffee "experience." Using that model, Starbucks had blossomed from 119 stores to around 15,000. But when the economy started to tank, people balked at spending four dollars for a fancy cup of coffee. And it wasn't only the economy. Starbucks had expanded so quickly, and its stores had begun to look so similar to one another, that instead of being perceived as a cozy neighborhood hangout, they were now viewed as McDonald's for yuppies. On top of that, rivals like Dunkin' Donuts and McDonald's itself began rolling out their own premium coffee drinks at lower prices than Starbucks'.

Schultz launched a full-court press to change the company, which he outlined in a series of memos called "Transformation Agenda Communications" that he emailed to the company's 172,000 employees. The first of these communications laid out the basics: "The success of Starbucks rests on the emotional connection we have with each other and with our customers. . . . In refocusing our Company, we are going to play to our strengths—to what has made Starbucks and the Starbucks experience so unique."[2]

Schultz's plan was many-faceted, but a lot of attention was paid to the scent of fresh coffee, the sound of beans being ground, the hiss of new espresso machines, and the taste of coffee brewed in smaller batches—in other words, to intensifying the experience that had attracted customers in the first place. At the same time, Schultz sought new ways to entice people to stay and sip. He added Wi-Fi to the stores. He tested a $1.00 cup of coffee. He ran specials and created discount cards for frequent drinkers.

Meanwhile, faced with plummeting stock prices and sales, Schultz closed six hundred stores in the United States and laid off thousands of employees. That meant he'd have to work extra hard to bolster the morale of those who remained. In his first emailed "Transformation Agenda," he had invited employees to write him back with suggestions for the transformation. Within a month he had received more than two thousand responses. In his fourth communication he wrote, "I can feel your passion and commitment to the company, to our customers and to one another. I also thank you for all your ideas and suggestions . . . keep them coming."[3]

Six weeks after his first communication on the subject, Schultz was ready to show America that Starbucks was changing. He did it with a masterful stroke of marketing: He closed all 7,100 Starbucks stores in the United States for three hours on a Tuesday evening, "to conduct a nationwide hands-on espresso training experience" for Starbucks employees.[4] You can bet it got the media's attention. In the following months, Schultz brought the Starbucks customer into the transformation process, launching a MyStarbucksIdea.com website where people could offer suggestions and follow up to see if the company had implemented them. To his credit, Schultz frequently and publicly took responsibility for the too-rapid expansion of the company and for allowing Starbucks stores to become, in his own words, "sterile."[5]

Two years later, the strategy appeared to be working. The flagging economy still posed a problem, but in January 2010, Starbucks reported that its first-quarter earnings (including the holiday season) were up 4 percent from the previous year, and same-store sales were up 4 percent as well. Several new stores in the company's birthplace, Seattle, embodied Schultz's vow to revive his employees' entrepreneurial spirit. As reported in the *New York Times*, Schultz had urged the Seattle employees to "break the rules and do things for yourself." Battling the cookie-cutter image was crucial. At the Starbucks in Seattle's University Village, a long table made out of a fallen ash tree was fitted with electrical outlets so students could study together. At another store on Capitol Hill, employees deposited used coffee grounds in a bucket outside so neighbors could take the grounds for composting (Capitol Hill is known for its avid gardeners). Inside, wildflowers in antique jugs continued the garden theme.

Focusing on local tastes was part of the transformation agenda as well. When Starbucks had ballooned to thousands of stores, its regional executives had been assigned according to time zone. Yet people's coffee preferences varied according to geography: Folks in the Southwest liked iced drinks, Pacific Northwesterners preferred espresso, and so forth. So Starbucks changed its regions to encompass geographical groups with similar tastes rather than time zones. In addition, Starbucks buyers were directed to purchase more small-batch coffees to appeal to consumers who prefer "artisanal" brews.

As for employee input, Schultz told the *Times* that he planned to open stores in other cities that would feature salvaged furniture and paintings by local artists, all presumably selected by employees. Next time you're in a Starbucks, take a look around and see if the Transformation Agenda has come to your neighborhood.[6]

POWER #27

Be Your Own Pundit

When I first began conducting focus groups, I would watch the videotapes of the sessions afterward, as much as six hours' worth at a time. I saw the way I interacted with a group of fifteen or twenty strangers and how they all interacted with one another. It was an intensive course in communication. Engaging people on every topic, from products to politicians to the most serious legal matters, I saw how the same principles applied everywhere. Combined with what I knew about marketing, I gained what I believe are unusual insights into the art and craft of persuasion. The most effective of these insights have been distilled into the powers in this book.

Most of the conversations you have in your lifetime will be open to influence by these powers. While you need to read the book in order to start using them, the way to get really good at the powers is to review them after a meeting, sales pitch, speech, presentation, or even a simple conversation with your spouse. The twenty-seventh power of persuasion is to reflect on the other twenty-six powers when a persuasion experience is fresh in your mind. That's when your learning curve will be the steepest.

So be your own pundit. Review both your successes and your failures, and try to figure out what worked and what didn't. After a meeting with your boss, ask yourself, "When she said that, what was she doing? What chapter did that fit into? What didn't she do? How could I have redirected the conversation? How could I have kept it simple and soothed her ego?" If you asked for a raise and got it, review the powers and ask yourself which ones you used. If you didn't get the raise, think about which powers you could have used that might have helped.

I've made every mistake in this book more than once, but because I'm my own pundit I've been able to learn from those mistakes. I still mentally review all my important "performances." After I've been in a meeting, I ask myself, "Did I stick to the goal? Did I keep it simple? Did I play to their predispositions? Did I arm my advocates? Did I use a couple of numbers?" To this day, there is one power that regularly catches me off guard. I know too much about my own business—persuasion—so when I'm with a client I'll occasionally forget about the goal and jump directly to persuasion tactics. Sticking to the goal is the biggest challenge for most people, and it's at the core of successful persuasion, which is why "Focus on the Goal" is the first power in this book.

I want to leave you with a list of performance tips you can use whenever you're persuading. They're adapted from the tips I ask clients to memorize before we go to trial. We call it Testimony 101, and it helps people on the witness stand come across as poised, confident, and sincere. When you are persuading a group, the same rules apply. I've added a few extra tips that witnesses can't use, but you can.

Persuasion Performance 101

- Know your message—the thirty-second story.
- Relax and breathe.
- If you need to fidget, wiggle your toes.
- Don't clench your hands.
- Don't assume the others in the room understand your profession. Don't talk over their heads. Explain your terms.
- Don't use acronyms unless the group knows what they mean.
- Let others finish a question before you start to answer.
- When you answer, look at the person asking the question.
- If you don't understand a question, ask for clarification. It's better to play ignorant and seem like a quick learner than to pretend to know something that you don't.
- If you need to think about an answer, cast your eyes down, not up. Looking down appears thoughtful; looking up seems like you're searching.
- It's okay to pause when you're giving a presentation. To

the speaker, a pause can feel like confusion, but to the audience a pause appears thoughtful.

- Silence is better than "hmm," "uh huh," or "you know."
- In one-on-one meetings, if it's appropriate, end with touch—a handshake, a pat on the back, a hug. It's inclusive and reassuring.

NOTES

3. Soothe or Sidestep Other Egos

1 *60 Minutes*, "Charlie Rose Interviews: The Man Who Helped Reinvent Las Vegas," www.cbsnews.com/stories/2009/04/10/60minutes/main4935567_page4.shtml?tag=contentMain;contentBody.

5. Make Your Weakness Your Strength

1 Peggy Noonan, George H. W. Bush's Acceptance Address at the 1988 Republican National Convention, August 18, 1988.

2 Rob Turner, "In Learning Hurdles, Lessons for Success," *New York Times*, November 23, 2003.

12. Own the Language

1 "Green Is Universal: Grindzilla!" *Forecast Earth*, Weather Channel (aired 11/17/2009), http://climate.weather.com/video/index.html?collection=247; Jeff Fleener, "Grindzilla Technology Showcase: A Unique Niche," *WHEN: Waste Handling Equipment News*, May 8, 2008, www.wastehandling.com/ME2/Audiences/dirmod.asp?sid=&nm=&type=Publishing&mod=Publications%3A%3AArticle&mid=8F3A7027421841978F18BE895F87F791&id=8D64E4C4FB6A4D27B2E445ADBB0AD809&tier=4.

2 ServiceUntitled.com, "Interview: Robert Stephens—Founder of the Geek Squad," February 12, 2007, www.serviceuntitled.com/interview-robert-stephens-founder-of-the-geek-squad/2007/02/12.

3 "The Geek Squad Story: A Short Video on the History of the Geek Squad," Google Videos, http://video.google.com/videoplay?docid=7519770909905424825#.

4 Ibid.

5 Josephine Moulds, "Business Profile: Robert Stephens, Geek Squad Founder," *Telegraph*, August 25, 2007, www.telegraph.co.uk/finance/markets/2814604/Business-profile-Robert-Stephens-Geek-Squad-founder.html.

6 "The Geek Squad Story."

15. Get Third-Party Validation

1 Michael Hart, "People: Empowering the Consumer" (interview with J.D. Power), *San Fernando Valley Business Journal*, June 11, 2001, http://findarticles.com/p/articles/mi_hb274/is_12_6/ai_n28848124/.

16. Get a Couple of Numbers

1 StateMaster.com, www.statemaster.com/index.php.

17. Arm Your Advocates

1 CNN, "'If It Doesn't Fit, You Must Acquit': Defense Attacks Prosecution's Case; Says Simpson Was Framed," September 28, 1995, www.cnn.com/US/OJ/daily/9-27/8pm.

2 CNN, "Juror Says Key Witnesses Lacked Credibility," October 4, 1995, www.cnn.com/US/OJ/daily/9510/10-04/moran/transcript.html.

18. Aim for the Undecideds

1 Peter Keating, "Those Mysterious Undecided Voters, and Why Obama Should Be Worried About Them," *New York*, October 16, 2008, http://nymag.com/daily/intel/2008/10/those_mysterious_undecided_vot.html.

2 Moms for McCain, "Who Are the Undecided Voters?" June 3, 2008, http://moms4mccain.blogspot.com/2008/06/who-are-undecided-voters.html.

3 Daily Gusto, "Who Are the Undecideds?" August 30, 2004, www.daily gusto.com/blog/archives/2004/08/who-are-the-undecideds.php.

4 Andrea Hopkins, "Who Are the Undecided in This Historic U.S. Vote?" *National Post*, October 29, 2008, www.nationalpost.com/news/world/uselection/story.html?id=917151.

5 Ezra Klein, "Undecided Voters? Studies Show That Most Actually Have Chosen a Candidate," *Los Angeles Times*, October 12, 2008, www.latimes.com/news/opinion/la-oe-klein12-2008oct12,0,6236237.story.

6 Ibid.

7 Denise Gellene, "Undecided? It's More Partisan Than You Think," *Los Angeles Times*, August 22, 2008, http://articles.latimes.com/2008/aug/22/science/sci-undecided22.

8 Project Implicit, "General Information," www.projectimplicit.net/generalinfo.php.

19. Avoid Absolutes and Hypotheticals

1 Roger Simon, "Questions That Kill Candidates' Careers," Politico, April 20, 2007, www.politico.com/news/stories/0407/3617.html.

2 Debate Transcript, October 13, 1988, The Second Bush-Dukakis Presidential Debate, copyright © 2004 by the Commission on Presidential Debates. All rights reserved.

3 Don Aucoin, "Blitzer Tries to Corner Clinton," *Boston Globe*, A10, February 7, 1998.

20. Learn How to Use Silence

1 Bob Dotson, "Better Writing at the Speed of Spot News," www.rtnda.org.

21. Get Physical

1 *Dennis Miller Live* (interview with Jon Stewart), June 9, 2000, www.youtube.com/watch?v=HE42PMdesJg&feature=related.

24. Challenge Bad Ideas by Challenging the Details

1 HealthVote.org, "Tobacco Tax: AdWatch," November 19, 2006, www.healthvote.org/index.php/adwatch/analysis/C37/koop.

2 SmartVoter.org, "Proposition 77," November 8, 2005, www.smartvoter.org/2005/11/08/ca/state/prop/77.

3 Evan Halper and Jordan Rau, "Political Ads Often Aim to Confuse," *Los Angeles Times*, November 6, 2005.

4 Harrison Sheppard, "Prop. 77 Con: Measure Power Grab by GOP," *Los Angeles Daily News*, October 13, 2005.

5 *The Sacramento Bee*, "Yes on 11 Rolls Out TV Ad (Without Governor Listed as Top Donor)," October 14, 2008, www.sacbee.com/static/weblogs/capitolalertlatest/2008/10/yes-on-11-rolls.html.

26. Don't Change, "Adapt"

1 Ylan Q. Mui, "Franchises Sue KFC over Shift to Grilled Chicken," *Washington Post*, January 9, 2010, www.washingtonpost.com/wp-dyn/content/article/2010/01/08/AR2010010803682.html.

2 Howard Schultz, "Transformation Agenda Communication #1," January 7, 2008, www.starbucks.com/aboutus/pressdesc.asp?id=814.

3 Howard Schultz, "Transformation Agenda Communication #4," February 4, 2008, http://news.starbucks.com/article_display.cfm?article_id=70.

4 Howard Schultz, "Transformation Agenda Communication #6," February 11, 2008, www.starbucks.com/aboutus/pressdesc.asp?id=830.

5 Jenny Wiggins, "The Trouble with Starbucks," *Financial Times*, December 12, 2008, www.ft.com/cms/s/2/aa9831ce-c266-11dd-a350-000077b07658.html.

6 Claire Cain Miller, "Now at Starbucks: A Rebound," *New York Times*, January 20, 2010, www.nytimes.com/2010/01/21/business/21sbux.html.

ABOUT THE AUTHORS

Chris St. Hilaire is a Pollie Award–winning consultant who has developed communications strategies for more than twenty years. In 2007, his firm was recognized at the American Business Awards as one of the nation's "most innovative" companies.

Chris is the author of the book *27 Powers of Persuasion: Simple Strategies to Seduce Audiences and Win Allies* (Prentice Hall Press), which CNBC recently called "powerful new ideas on how to get others to follow you."

As a message consultant for some of the most high-profile cases in America, St. Hilaire advises many of the world's largest corporations on litigation and public messaging.

His column, The Word Consultant, is published monthly in *Smart Business* magazine. Chris has also been the featured speaker at Google and Microsoft Corporation, and provided legal and political commentary in *USA Today* and on national news broadcasts, such as NBC, C-SPAN, and Fox News. He has been a featured guest on *Fox and Friends* morning show. In addition, Jury Impact and M4 Strategies have been featured in the *Los Angeles Times*, as well as other national newspapers and publications.

Chris has served as political director to the former California State Assembly Minority Leader and as chief strategist and message specialist for the U.S. Chamber of Commerce and other national political organizations, including Presidential and U.S. Senate campaigns.

Lynette Padwa is the author of *Quick, Answer Me Before I Forget the Question: Everything You Need to Know About Turning 50*; *Say the Magic Words: How to Get What You Want from the People Who Have What You Need*; and the bestselling *Everything You Pretend to Know and Are Afraid Someone Will Ask*. She has collaborated on numerous books, including *Moses on Management: 50 Leadership Lessons from the Greatest Manager of All Time* (with David Baron). She lives in Los Angeles.